STRATEGIC FORCES

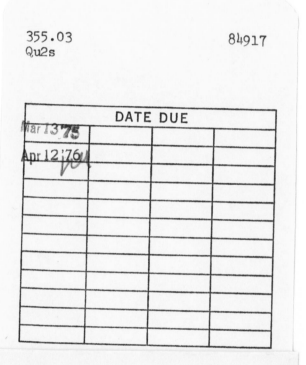

ALTON H. QUANBECK *and* BARRY M. BLECHMAN

STRATEGIC FORCES
Issues for the Mid-Seventies

A Staff Paper

THE BROOKINGS INSTITUTION
Washington, D.C.

Copyright © 1973 by
THE BROOKINGS INSTITUTION
1775 Massachusetts Avenue, N.W., Washington, D.C. 20036

Library of Congress Cataloging in Publication Data:
Quanbeck, Alton H   1926–
  Strategic forces: issues for the mid-seventies.
  (Studies in defense policy)
  Includes bibliographical references.
    1. United States—Military policy.   2. Atomic weapons.
I. Blechman, Barry M., joint author.   II. Title.   III. Series.
UA23.Q35   355.03'3073   73-1088
ISBN 0-8157-7283-1 (pbk)

9 8 7 6 5 4 3 2 1

THE BROOKINGS INSTITUTION is an independent organization devoted to nonpartisan research, education, and publication in economics, government, foreign policy, and the social sciences generally. Its principal purposes are to aid in the development of sound public policies and to promote public understanding of issues of national importance.

The Institution was founded on December 8, 1927, to merge the activities of the Institute for Government Research, founded in 1916, the Institute of Economics, founded in 1922, and the Robert Brookings Graduate School of Economics and Government, founded in 1924.

The Board of Trustees is responsible for the general administration of the Institution, while the immediate direction of the policies, program, and staff is vested in the President, assisted by an advisory committee of the officers and staff. The by-laws of the Institution state, "It is the function of the Trustees to make possible the conduct of scientific research, and publication, under the most favorable conditions, and to safeguard the independence of the research staff in the pursuit of their studies and in the publication of the results of such studies. It is not a part of their function to determine, control, or influence the conduct of particular investigations or the conclusions reached."

The President bears final responsibility for the decision to publish a manuscript as a Brookings book or staff paper. In reaching his judgment on the competence, accuracy, and objectivity of each study, the President is advised by the director of the appropriate research program and weighs the views of a panel of expert outside readers who report to him in confidence on the quality of the work. Publication of a work signifies that it is deemed to be a competent treatment worthy of public consideration; such publication does not imply endorsement of conclusions or recommendations contained in the study.

The Institution maintains its position of neutrality on issues of public policy in order to safeguard the intellectual freedom of the staff. Hence interpretations or conclusions in Brookings publications should be understood to be solely those of the author or authors and should not be attributed to the Institution, to its trustees, officers, or other staff members, or to the organizations that support its research.

FOREWORD

Strategic nuclear weapons are an essential part of this country's military forces, even though their main purpose is to ensure that they never have to be used. In fiscal 1973 they account for slightly more than one-fifth of the Defense Department's budget, or a total of $17 billion. Despite the strategic arms limitation agreements reached with the Soviet Union in 1972, spending for strategic weapons is likely to increase to nearly $22 billion by fiscal 1978 and to remain at about that level through the end of the decade. As an aid to understanding this apparent paradox, this paper—the fourth in the Brookings Studies in Defense Policy series—examines the major issues that determine the nature and cost of the U.S. strategic forces, how those forces are interrelated, and what they contribute to strategic deterrence.

The authors discuss the strategic arms limitation agreements and the continuing negotiations with the Soviet Union, strategic doctrine, the military balance between the United States and its possible adversaries, the foreign policy implications of changes in strategic posture, and domestic political and bureaucratic influences. Examining each part of the strategic force—land-based missiles, sea-based missiles, bombers, antiballistic missile defenses, and air defenses—the authors describe existing plans and programs and project their cost through the end of the 1970s. They also consider the potential costs and benefits of alternative programs and some of the technical factors that would affect choices among them.

Using a range of illustrative strategic postures for the United States, the authors indicate how the strategic arms budget might be reduced within the confines of existing policy. They emphasize, however, that deciding whether to obtain or to do without a particular strategic weapon rests on more than a quantitative analysis of costs and effectiveness. Ultimately, any decision affecting strategic force levels depends on American policymakers' judgments of the value of redundancy and flexibility in the strategic force, and on their assessment of the political consequences of changing the nation's military posture as it is perceived by allies and possible adversaries abroad.

Alton H. Quanbeck is a senior fellow and director of the Defense Analysis project in the Brookings Foreign Policy Studies program. Barry M. Blechman is a senior fellow on the Defense Analysis staff.

The Brookings Institution wishes to thank members of its Defense Analysis Advisory Board—James R. Killian, George H. Quester, Stanley R. Resor, General Matthew B. Ridgway, and Charles Rossotti—for their helpful comments on this paper. Others who gave generously of their time to comment on the manuscript include Andrew P. Borden, Brigadier General Arnold W. Braswell, Commander James J. Martin, Robert C. Moot, Thomas R. Pickering, K. Wayne Smith, Vice Admiral Stansfield Turner, Seymour Weiss, and Archie L. Wood. The authors are also grateful for suggestions of their colleagues at Brookings, Henry D. Owen and Edward R. Fried, and for the editorial assistance of James D. Farrell. Of course the authors themselves are responsible for any shortcomings in the analysis.

The Institution acknowledges the assistance of the Ford Foundation, which provided a grant in support of its defense and foreign policy studies. The views expressed herein are solely those of the authors and should not be attirbuted to the Ford Foundation or to the trustees, officers, or other staff members of the Brookings Institution.

KERMIT GORDON
President

March 1973
Washington, D.C.

CONTENTS

Tables

Figure

CHAPTER ONE

INTRODUCTION

In May 1972, two and one-half years of negotiations between the United States and the Soviet Union were concluded successfully with the signing of the strategic arms limitation agreements by President Richard M. Nixon and Secretary Leonid Brezhnev. The two accords, impressive in their scope as well as in their detail, were hailed by most observers as landmarks in the evolution of U.S.–Soviet relations. In the words of the President's national security adviser, Henry Kissinger:

For the first time, two great powers, deeply divided by their divergent values, philosophies, and social systems have agreed to restrain the very armaments on which their national survival depends. . . . The final verdict must wait on events, but there is at least reason to hope that these accords represent a major break in the pattern of suspicion, hostility, and confrontation which has dominated U.S.–Soviet relations for a generation.[1]

Almost immediately, however, it became apparent that substantial reductions in spending for nuclear armaments were not among the benefits that could be expected from the agreements. Both superpowers made clear that the strategic arms race would continue, though in somewhat altered directions. Soviet officials suggested that they intended to continue weapon development programs within the bounds prescribed by the treaties and apparently have carried out that intention.[2] The secretary of defense, the chairman of the Joint Chiefs of Staff, and other American military representatives indicated that their support for the arms control arrangements was contingent on continued weapon modernization.

1. Congressional Briefing by Dr. Henry A. Kissinger (Office of the White House Press Secretary, June 15, 1972; processed), included in *Strategic Arms Limitations Agreements*, Hearings before the Senate Committee on Foreign Relations, 92 Cong. 2 sess. (1972), p. 400.
2. *New York Times*, October 1, 1972.

Table 1-1. Projected Costs of U.S. Strategic Forces and Civil Defense, Fiscal Years 1973–80

Total obligational authority in billions of fiscal 1974 dollars

Component	1973	1974	1975	1976	1977	1978	1979	1980
Land-based missiles	3.0	3.1	2.7	2.3	2.1	2.0	1.6	1.2
Sea-based missiles	4.1	4.7	5.2	5.6	5.6	5.6	5.8	5.9
Bombers and tankers[a]	5.6	5.6	5.6	6.9	7.5	7.9	8.2	8.4
Antiballistic missile defenses	1.5	1.3	1.2	1.1	1.1	1.1	1.1	1.1
Air defense, warning, and control	3.2	3.2	3.7	4.1	4.6	4.7	5.0	5.0
Civil defense	0.1	0.1	0.1	0.1	0.1	0.1	0.1	0.1
Total[a]	17.5	18.0	18.5	20.1	21.0	21.4	21.8	21.7

Source: Authors' estimates based on data in various Defense Department publications and in hearings on the fiscal 1972 and 1973 Defense Department budgets before the Senate and House Armed Services and Appropriations Committees.

a. Excludes incremental costs of the war in Southeast Asia.

On their surface these developments are confusing. On the one hand, the superpowers have achieved the most comprehensive arms control agreements since the Second World War. On the other hand, despite this achievement the strategic arms race has not been stopped and spending continues at high levels. Moreover, the weapon development programs now under way promise to require even higher spending levels in future years. If the administration carries out its plans, as revealed in congressional testimony by Defense Department officials, spending for strategic forces is likely to increase in real terms from around $17.5 billion in fiscal 1973 to $21 billion in fiscal 1977 and to remain at roughly that level through the end of the decade.[3] The costs of strategic forces are projected through fiscal 1980 in Table 1-1.

To understand this seeming paradox—the contrast between progress toward arms control and continuing increases in spending for strategic forces —one must explore a wide range of subjects. First there are the strategic arms limitation agreements themselves, and what they do and do not proscribe. Then there are the manifold factors that determine the U.S. strategic posture. These may be grouped into four broad categories:

Doctrine. That is, a definition of the purposes of nuclear weapons, how they would be used (if at all), and the degree of confidence required in planning for various contingencies.

3. These estimates include a proportional share of indirect support costs. For details of the methodology, see App. E.

Military requirements. Given a strategic doctrine and projections of the military capabilities of potential adversaries, it is possible to estimate the specific military requirements for carrying out the objectives stated in the doctrine. These requirements determine force levels—the kinds and quantities of weapons—and modernization—the rate at which new weapons are developed and produced and older weapons retired.

Political requirements. The nation's strategic posture—the military image it projects to friends and foes alike—is probably the most important single element determining how other states expect the United States to behave in various eventualities and consequently in determining the U.S. position in world affairs. The trends foreign states perceive in U.S. military strength, particularly in relation to trends in the military posture of potential adversaries, are said to have profound implications for the future success of U.S. foreign policy. A strong and growing relative strategic capability will, it is argued, provide incentives for adversaries to negotiate for mutually beneficial solutions to outstanding problems. It will reassure allies of U.S. capabilities and willingness to come to their defense, if need be, thereby reinforcing other factors strengthening the alliance. Finally, it will cause third parties to treat U.S. policies with respect and to be more amenable to U.S. foreign undertakings. On the other hand, a declining relative strategic posture will encourage hostile initiatives by potential adversaries, cause allies to worry about U.S. intentions, and provide little incentive for third nations to accommodate U.S. preferences. Depending on the importance attached to these political factors, decisions on force levels and modernization may well exceed requirements based on purely military calculations.

Other factors. Finally, strategic posture decisions may reflect bureaucratic inertia, domestic political considerations, and the outcome of interpersonal and organizational disputes within the defense policy community.

This paper is intended to aid in understanding the reasons for continuing increases in spending for strategic forces. Concurrently it assesses alternatives to existing plans for force levels and modernization and explains the tradeoffs they imply between spending and imputed benefits in terms of the four considerations listed above.

After a brief discussion of strategic doctrine, the strategic arms limitation talks, and the military capabilities of potential adversaries, the paper focuses on specific strategic force structure issues. It examines the components of the U.S. strategic posture, discusses administration plans regarding their future and the critical factors bearing on those plans, and suggests possible alternative courses. The conclusions consider several aggregated budgetary options and the factors determining choices among them. They seek both to define needs under the doctrine of "strategic sufficiency" and to indicate the additional forces called for to meet other political and bureaucratic requirements.

CHAPTER TWO

FACTORS IN FORCE PLANNING

As they are now structured, U.S. strategic forces consist of six elements: land-based intercontinental ballistic missiles (ICBMs); submarine-launched ballistic missiles (SLBMs); manned bombers and their associated refueling tankers; antiballistic missile defenses (ABMs); air defenses; and warning, surveillance, and command and control systems.

The first three components make up the U.S. strategic offensive capability and are known as the Triad.

ABM and air defenses—the strategic defensive forces—play a secondary though not inexpensive role in the U.S. strategic posture. Since large-scale defenses of the American urban/industrial base have been ruled out by existing strategic doctrine, these forces are confined to protecting fixed land-based forces and the National Command Authority in Washington, and to defending against light or accidental attacks.

Warning and surveillance networks and command and control systems are essential to effective functioning of all the other forces. Because these systems are numerous, diverse in purpose, and usually highly classified, they are not examined closely in this study.

Strategic Doctrine

Current planning for the strategic forces is based on the doctrine of "strategic sufficiency." In articulating this policy, President Nixon accepted the basic premise underlying strategic force planning in previous administrations—that the fundamental purpose of strategic forces is to deter nuclear war by maintaining a secure retaliatory capability—but he added other criteria, which, he said, "take into account political factors and a broader set of military factors."[1]

While many of the precepts of strategic sufficiency enjoy widespread support within the defense policy community, others are contentious in varying degrees. Debates about them reflect differing viewpoints concerning the appropriate strategic posture for the United States. How these issues are resolved will determine—within the general context of strategic sufficiency—which of several possible alternative U.S. force structures is adopted.

Secure Retaliatory Capability

Advocates of strategic sufficiency argue, as did those of its predecessor doctrines, that the actual physical defense of the nation from strategic nuclear attack is too risky, too costly, and too likely to encourage unstable relations between the United States and its adversaries to be a worthwhile policy. Instead, they propose to deter a nuclear attack on this country, or on states that it is unambiguously committed to defend, by confronting potential attackers with the certainty that, should they attack, they would in turn suffer unacceptable levels of destruction. The central precept of the doctrine is, therefore, that the U.S. strategic force must be capable of absorbing an attack by any combination of potential aggressors, and of inflicting massive damage to the attacker's industry and population in return. This capability must be made known to potential adversaries, and it must be unambiguous. As the President has said, "Our forces must be maintained at a level sufficient to make it clear that even an all-out surprise attack on the United States by the USSR would not cripple our capability to retaliate."[2]

To ensure confidence in the U.S. retaliatory capability, planners generally have relied on two corollaries. First, in calculating the ability of the force to carry out the retaliatory mission, they use the most pessimistic assessment of Soviet capabilities and circumstances surrounding the outbreak of hostilities. Second, an independent retaliatory capability is maintained in the three separate offensive systems—land-based intercontinental ballistic missiles, submarine-launched ballistic missiles, and manned bombers—that compose the Triad. Because of their different modes of bas-

---

1. *U.S. Foreign Policy for the 1970's: The Emerging Structure of Peace*, A Report to the Congress by Richard M. Nixon, President of the United States (February 9, 1972), p. 175.

2. *Ibid.*, p. 176.

ing and penetration, the survivability of each component is considered to be relatively independent of that of the others. Secretary of Defense Melvin R. Laird noted that the advantages of this arrangement are "to provide a hedge against enemy technological breakthroughs or unforeseen operational failures . . . and to complicate Soviet . . . strategic planning."[3]

A wide consensus among American strategic analysts supports the idea that deterrence through secure retaliatory capability is the primary function of strategic forces. A minority view deserves mention, however. This approach, which can be called "defense emphasis," became quite prominent during the debate over building the Safeguard antiballistic missile system during the late 1960s. It disputes the basic premise of strategic sufficiency—that the best way to prevent nuclear war is to maintain the vulnerability of each side to the other's retaliatory forces. As Donald G. Brennan, perhaps the foremost advocate of defense emphasis, put it: "If technology and international politics provided absolutely no alternative, one might reluctantly accept a MAD [mutual assured destruction] posture. But to think of it as desirable, for instance, as a clearly preferred goal of our arms control negotiations . . . is bizarre."[4]

As an alternative, the defense-emphasis school advocates a policy based on the protection of U.S. population and industry through the massive deployment of antimissile and aircraft defenses, combined with civil defenses of major proportions. Only by minimizing the potential destruction of an opponent's attack, it is claimed, can such an attack be deterred. Supporters of this school view deterrence through secure retaliatory capability as inherently unstable, unproved, and the product of wishful thinking.[5]

Military Flexibility

An important planning concept that President Nixon has added to U.S. strategic doctrine, and a contentious one at that, is the structuring of strategic forces so that they can respond in a variety of ways to various military

3. *Annual Defense Department Report, FY 1973*, Statement of Secretary of Defense Melvin R. Laird before the Senate Armed Services Committee on the FY 1973 Defense Budget and FY 1973–1977 Program (February 15, 1972), p. 66.

4. *Strategic Arms Limitation Agreements*, Hearings before the Senate Committee on Foreign Relations, 92 Cong. 2 sess. (1972), p. 187.

5. For a discussion of this view, see Donald G. Brennan, "The Case for Population Defenses," *Why ABM?* (Pergamon Press, 1969); for a discussion of the SALT agreements from this perspective, see Brennan, "When the SALT Hit the Fan," *National Review* (June 23, 1972), pp. 685–92.

contingencies. In calling for flexibility, the President stated: "No President should be left with only one strategic course of action, particularly that of ordering the mass destruction of enemy civilians and facilities. Given the range of possible political–military situations which could conceivably confront us ... we must be able to respond at levels appropriate to the situation."[6]

According to this view, American leaders should not have to choose between capitulation and ordering an all-out attack. Its proponents argue that the Soviet Union could attack one element of the Triad, say land-based missiles, and effectively destroy it while using only a small part of its own strategic force. The USSR then could threaten to destroy American cities if a response were mounted against Soviet population centers. In this contingency, under previous targeting plans and weapon capabilities, the President would be left with a very difficult choice. Proponents of a flexible response contend that the President should be able to order a similar attack on Soviet land-based missiles or some other set of military targets, thereby maintaining the relative immunity of U.S. population centers.

To gain flexibility the administration has undertaken or proposed a variety of programs, including Command Data Buffer, a series of measures designed to give land-based missiles the ability to be retargeted quickly and flexibly; the development of new warheads with greater accuracy and higher yields for use against well-protected military targets; and the development of new delivery systems such as maneuvering reentry vehicles and submarine-launched cruise missiles. Details of some of these programs are presented in Chapter 3.

Objections to these proposals center on plans to develop warheads with greater accuracy. Opponents argue that, despite official U.S. denials, Soviet planners would have to view the development of such weapons as steps toward the attainment of a first strike capability by the United States—that is, the ability to destroy Soviet retaliatory forces in a preemptive attack. To do otherwise would be to take American statements on faith, a position no Soviet defense official is likely to accept. Consequently it is argued that development of these weapons would destabilize the U.S.–Soviet strategic relationship by putting pressure on the Soviet Union to take counter-measures, such as the development of antiballistic missile systems.

Some question the wisdom of obtaining strategic flexibility in and of it-

6. *U.S. Foreign Policy for the 1970's*, p. 157.

self. To these critics, any measure that seemed to diminish the potential destruction likely to be suffered in a nuclear war would increase the chance that such a war will actually occur. Since any nuclear war would be extremely costly, they consider such measures undesirable.[7]

Stability in Crises

The United States has an interest in reducing the USSR's incentives to strike first in a confrontation. In part this is to be done by introducing into U.S. force planning the elements of flexibility just discussed. Knowledge that the United States could respond in kind rather than choose between surrender and massive retaliation, it is said, will reduce the USSR's willingness to stage less than an all-out attack.

Also contributing to stability is the USSR's knowledge that it would suffer approximately the same damage whether the United States struck first or in retaliation. If the anticipated damage levels were very different, the Soviet Union, fearing a U.S. first strike during a crisis, could be tempted to strike first itself in order to reduce the expected damage—even though that damage would be great. Therefore the United States seeks to minimize the difference between its first and second strike capabilities by making all parts of its strategic offensive forces relatively invulnerable.

Political Factors: Maintaining a Balance

The final criterion incorporated in the doctrine of strategic sufficiency is that a rough balance should be evident between the strategic capabilities of the United States and its possible adversaries. In the President's words:

Sufficiency requires forces that are adequate in quantity and have the qualitative characteristics to maintain a stable strategic balance despite technological change. Capabilities of both the U.S. and USSR have reached a point where our programs need not be driven by fear of minor quantitative imbalances. The Soviet Union cannot be permitted, however, to establish a significant numerical advantage in overall offensive and defensive forces.[8]

7. The new weapons recommended to increase the flexibility of U.S. strategic forces are discussed, and contrasting views presented, in *New York Times*, August 9, 1972, and *Washington Post*, August 13 and August 29, 1972.

8. *U.S. Foreign Policy for the 1970's*, p. 187.

The importance of maintaining a rough balance is said to lie in preventing coercion or intimidation of the United States or its allies. If a substantial imbalance should develop, a psychological atmosphere would be created in which the Soviet Union could wrest various concessions from the United States, even if the United States maintained a secure retaliatory capability. Proponents of balance point to the Cuban missile crisis as evidence of the importance of this factor, arguing that the United States was able to force withdrawal of the Soviet missiles because of its clear strategic superiority at that time. Should the strategic balance be reversed in the future, it is argued, a similar retreat could be forced on the United States.

The balance criterion is used to justify the maintenance of numbers of strategic systems comparable to those of the Soviet Union, though some of them may contribute only marginally to U.S. retaliatory capability. Similarly, a vigorous weapon modernization program is justified in part by the political benefits imputed to increasing strategic capabilities.

This criterion is probably the most contentious part of the doctrine of strategic sufficiency. Its most extreme critics are those who advocate a posture of "minimum deterrence." They assert that the destruction associated with any foreseeable U.S.–Soviet nuclear exchange would be so great that the behavior of the two states is likely to be independent of their relative capabilities, so long as mutual retaliatory capabilities are maintained. In brief, the risks are so great that neither superpower would be willing to take steps that could lead to a nuclear war. Holders of this view contend that the outcome of the Cuban missile crisis resulted less from the strategic balance than from the relative general purpose force capabilities the superpowers could bring to bear. One who makes such an assumption is likely to recommend strategic forces much smaller than those currently maintained by the United States.

Less extreme critics recognize the political implications of a gross imbalance but contend that simple force level comparisons are misleading. More important in their view are relative capabilities as measured by qualitative as well as quantitative factors. In addition, they see a rather loose relationship between capabilities and political consequences. Given the uncertainties inherent in strategic calculations, they would argue that fairly large imbalances could arise before political effects would be felt.[9]

9. For an excellent presentation of these views, see Benjamin S. Lambeth, "Deterrence in the MIRV Era," *World Politics*, Vol. 24 (January 1972), pp. 221–42.

Costs and Benefits

Of course another goal in designing strategic forces is to allocate resources where they offer the greatest payoff in meeting strategic objectives. If forces that make only marginal contributions are eliminated, the resources saved can be directed to more productive military uses or to civilian needs. It should be recognized, however, that the results of quantitative cost–benefit analyses depend heavily on subjective judgments regarding assumptions and relative values. Indeed the day-to-day debate on strategic forces does not concern objectives so much as it does the weight to be given various military and political risks, the margin of safety to be incorporated in planning assumptions, and the uncertainties inherent in the calculations.

The Strategic Arms Limitation Agreements

Successful completion of the first phase of the strategic arms limitation talks (SALT) has introduced new elements into U.S. strategic force planning. The agreements themselves, the debate attendant on their ratification, and the promise of future agreements are all significant factors.

The Agreements in Brief

The United States and the Soviet Union have concluded two separate accords. One, a formal treaty of unlimited duration, restricts the deployment of antiballistic missile systems (ABMs). In the key paragraph, each superpower agrees

not to deploy ABM systems for a defense of the territory of its country and not to provide a base for such a defense, and not to deploy ABM systems for defense of an individual region except as provided in Article III . . . .[10]

The exceptions are designed to accommodate ABM sites already in existence or under construction. Each nation is allowed to deploy and operate one site in defense of an offensive missile base, one site in defense of the national capital, and a test range. Each site is defined according to its area,

10. This and subsequent quotations from the agreements or associated documents are from *Military Implications of the Treaty on the Limitation of Anti-Ballistic Missile Systems and the Interim Agreement on Limitation of Strategic Offensive Arms*, Hearing before the Senate Armed Services Committee, 92 Cong. 2 sess. (1972).

permissible number of missile launchers, and the number, location, and type of radars that may be included. The ABM Treaty and associated documents also prohibit the development, testing, or deployment of new types of ABMs, such as those that would be based at sea or in the air, those that would be mobile on land, those with a rapid reload capability, and those based on radically new technologies. Each party also agrees not to transfer ABM systems or their components to other nations.

The signatories agree that observance of the treaty will be verified strictly by unilateral national means—that is, primarily by satellite reconnaissance. They have pledged not to interfere with verification systems either directly or through measures of deliberate concealment. The treaty provides for the establishment of a consultative commission to oversee implementation of the accord and to discuss amendments and further measures of strategic arms limitation. Finally, provision is made for review of the treaty at five-year intervals and for unilateral withdrawal from the treaty after a six-month notification period, if one of the signatories decides that its "supreme national interests" have been jeopardized.

The second accord, a less formal Interim Agreement of five-year duration, is designed to put a ceiling on strategic offensive weapon deployments while more durable and comprehensive limitations are worked out. The United States has linked the two accords. On May 9, 1972, Ambassador Gerard C. Smith, leader of the U.S. delegation to SALT, declared: "If an agreement providing for more complete strategic offensive arms limitations were not achieved within five years . . . it would constitute a basis for withdrawal from the ABM Treaty."[11]

The Interim Agreement establishes separate limits on the number of submarine-based and land-based strategic offensive missile launchers deployed by each signatory. The parties are prohibited from initiating construction of additional fixed ICBM launchers after July 1, 1972, and from converting "light" ICBMs to heavier missiles. With one exception, ballistic missile submarines and their associated launchers are limited to the number deployed or under construction at the time the agreement was signed. The exception, quite a significant one from the viewpoint of future negotiations, provides for the replacement of older ICBMs or SLBMs with an equal number of new submarine launchers.

11. *New York Times*, June 14, 1972. Smith's statement gained emphasis through its inclusion in the "unilateral statements" released by the White House in association with the texts of the agreements.

The Interim Agreement does not impose limits on aircraft, on theater nuclear weapons, or on sea-based or air-launched nonballistic missiles (for example, cruise missiles). Also excluded are mobile land-based ICBMs, though the United States has declared that it would consider the deployment of such a weapon as "inconsistent with the objectives of the agreement."[12] Most importantly, the Interim Agreement does not preclude continued technological rivalry and in fact specifically permits modernization and replacement of strategic offensive missiles and launchers, within the limits noted.

The Interim Agreement shares the safeguards and escape clauses of the ABM accord, providing for verification through unilateral national means, for use of the consultative commission, for further negotiations toward more extensive limitations, and for withdrawal if a signatory perceives that its supreme national interests are in danger.

Implications

The achievement of these accords, affecting weapons at the heart of each nation's security, is a major accomplishment and a dramatic symbol of the change in U.S.–Soviet relations. That the superpowers have been able to discuss these matters in a "candid and business like manner," and reach agreement despite major technical and political obstacles, demonstrates their mutual determination to reduce the risk of nuclear war. As was said in the joint communiqué issued at the end of President Nixon's visit to Moscow, "They are a concrete expression of the intention of the two sides to contribute to the relaxation of international tension and the strengthening of confidence between states. . . ."[13]

In combination the two agreements, while not completely halting U.S.–Soviet nuclear competition, are major steps toward controlling the strategic arms race. Most importantly, by explicitly pledging to forgo nationwide population defenses, the signatories have removed a significant threat to each other's deterrent and a major destabilizing element in the strategic balance. Of itself, this step should reduce the fears of each superpower as to its opponent's intentions and place loose boundaries around the competitive space. Although the strategic rivalry will continue, it is likely to do so within less uncertain bounds and in channels that have been fairly well de-

12. *Ibid.*
13. *New York Times*, May 30, 1972.

fined. Thus the "worst case" becomes less open ended and the possibility of an unrestrained arms race considerably lessened.

The Soviet pledge to forgo population defenses should be of particular import to Western military planners. For many years, some had maintained that the Soviet Union did not view nuclear weapons in the same terms as did the West. Specifically, it was argued that the USSR did not structure its strategic forces to maximize their deterrent capabilities, but rather was most interested in the "warfighting" capabilities of nuclear weapons. That is, it was argued that Soviet strategic planners saw no radical difference between strategic nuclear and conventional weapons, but viewed the former as an extension of long-range artillery. It was said that the pending deployment of more than 300 large ICBMs (SS-9s) supported this hypothesis, as did the deployment of the ABM system around Moscow. Continued deployment of the large ICBMs, if combined with further ABM construction (or perhaps the development of a similar capability by an upgrading of the so-called Tallinn air defense system), could enable the USSR to strike first against the United States and receive only minimal damage in retaliation.

The pledges contained in the ABM Treaty and the explicit limitations on ABMs and large ICBM deployments run counter to such views. It would seem that the Soviets do indeed think of nuclear forces in terms similar to those espoused by the United States. They would seem to recognize the destabilizing nature of population defenses; their objective would seem to be the establishment of a stable strategic equilibrium, based on the concept of deterrence through maintenance of secure retaliatory capabilities.

This is not to suggest that the Soviets have necessarily become firm believers in the merits of mutual deterrence. Clearly, many diverse views are held within the Soviet military and political bureaucracies, just as there are within our own. Even after the SALT accords, the writings of Soviet military specialists continue to emphasize the need for warfighting capabilities should deterrence fail. Consequently, one should not dismiss the possibility that the Soviets have accepted the ABM Treaty simply because of technological and financial constraints, without accepting the idea that mutual vulnerability leads to strategic stability.

While Soviet behavior would indicate acceptance of this idea, or at least that those who accept it prevailed in the internal debate over whether to sign the agreements, the evidence of continued dominance by those who would seek stable deterrence should not be overemphasized. Considering that the Soviet military inveighed openly against the very idea of holding talks on limiting strategic weapons in 1968 and 1969, opposition probably is still present and may gain greater influence in the future.

The SALT negotiations themselves may have played a part in educating the Soviets as to the precepts of American strategic doctrine and their value in reducing the risk of war and maintaining a stable strategic equilibrium. Ambassador Smith, the chief American negotiator, remarked on this process:

I think that the Soviets, as a result of the SALT negotiations, have moved toward accepting the concept of assured destruction. . . .

The best evidence that they are moving in that direction is their acceptance of these very low levels of ABMs which, in effect, indicates that they do not calculate that they can make a first strike and then handle a ragged retaliatory strike and keep it at tolerable levels.[14]

Just as the SALT negotiations were helpful in narrowing American uncertainty concerning Soviet strategic planning assumptions, the debate that accompanied ratification of the agreements in the United States Senate was instructive in revealing congressional notions of valid criteria for structuring and sizing strategic forces.

Little opposition to the ABM Treaty was voiced in the Congress, indicating a lack of support for the defense-emphasis approach. On the other hand, very heated debate accompanied Senate approval of the Interim Agreement on offensive weapons. Senatorial concerns centered on the provisions that permit the Soviets to deploy larger numbers of land-based and sea-based missile launchers than the United States. The Senate showed its concern by amending the resolution authorizing the agreement. The most pertinent part of the amendment, introduced by Senator Henry M. Jackson, read as follows:

. . . the Congress recognizes the principle of United States–Soviet Union equality reflected in the anti-ballistic missile treaty, and urges and requests the President to seek a future treaty that, *inter alia, would not limit the United States to levels of intercontinental strategic forces inferior to the limits provided for the Soviet Union.*[15]

Before accepting the Jackson amendment, the Senate rejected a less restrictive substitute motion by Senator J. William Fulbright. The latter stated:

The Congress supports continued negotiations to achieve further limitations on

14. *Military Implications of the Treaty . . . on Limitation of Strategic Offensive Arms*, Senate Hearing, pp. 383–84.

15. Amendment No. 1516, *Congressional Record*, daily ed., Sept. 14, 1972, p. S14870. (Italics added.)

offensive nuclear weapons systems with the Union of Soviet Socialist Republics *on the basis of overall equality, parity, and sufficiency, taking into account all relevant qualitative and quantitative factors. . . .*[16]

The Senate's action is likely to have significant consequences both for the U.S. position in future SALT negotiations and for unilateral decisions on force levels that will be made in the interim.

Future Negotiations

The second phase of SALT opened in Geneva in November 1972. While the agreements already attained are only first steps in the limitation of strategic armaments, they establish several important precedents and set the stage for more comprehensive arrangements.

One important precedent is the two nations' dependence on verification through unilateral national means. This reliance reflects the rapid advance in the technology of satellite reconnaissance and other forms of electronic surveillance in the past decade. It remains to be seen whether this technology will suffice to permit the application of unilateral verification to the more refined types of limitation likely to be included in Phase II SALT agreements. In any case, the use of satellites and other means of surveillance may have a profound effect on negotiations for other forms of arms control, a complete nuclear test ban being a prominent example.

A second important precedent is the provision allowing replacement of older land- or sea-based missiles with modern submarine-launched weapons. Conceivably, each side's land-based missile forces could become vulnerable in the future. The limitation on antiballistic missile defenses, coupled with improvements in missile accuracy and payload and with warhead proliferation, could lead to the attainment of a first strike capability against the land-based component in either the U.S. or the Soviet strategic force. One way to eliminate this potential problem would be to allow land-based missiles to be shifted to sea, perhaps at a less than one-to-one replacement ratio.

Hints of other topics likely to be prominent in subsequent SALT negotiations may be found in the "agreed" and "unilateral" interpretations issued with the Moscow accords.

The United States has insisted that more comprehensive limits on offensive systems be obtained within the five-year life of the Interim Agreement.

16. Amendment No. 1526, *ibid.* (Italics added.)

It has expressed specific concern about the lack of agreed limits on land-mobile ICBMs and Soviet medium- and intermediate-range land-based missiles (MR/IRBMs), about the testing of antiballistic missile systems, about the defense of early warning radars and, most significantly, about the lack of a precise differentiation between "heavy" and "light" missiles.

The last point is intimately related to what is likely to be the central U.S. negotiating objective. One reason the United States believed that it could grant the Soviet Union an advantage in numbers of launchers in the present agreements is that the U.S. technological lead and strategic bomber force provide other advantages, particularly in comparative numbers of warheads. Nevertheless, American strategic planners must assume that the USSR will make considerable progress in its own warhead technology during the period covered by the Interim Agreement. Given such a forecast, the United States is likely to press in future negotiations either for revisions in the launcher limitations so as to establish a strict quantitative parity, or for qualitative restrictions on deployed systems so as to limit the Soviet capability to match U.S. technology, or for a combination of the two.

On the Soviet side, negotiators in future SALT meetings are likely to be concerned with limiting the deployment of nuclear weapons by U.S. allies and with restricting U.S. access to foreign bases for strategic weapons; both topics were mentioned in a unilateral Soviet statement on the agreements. More importantly, the Soviets can be expected to seek limits on aircraft systems, which are now uncontrolled and are the component of the Triad in which the United States has the greatest advantage.

Finally, during past SALT rounds, Soviet negotiators have expressed concern with so-called forward based systems—that is, nuclear weapons that are generally considered tactical systems but that, because of their deployment in Europe and elsewhere, are capable of striking the Soviet homeland. In this area there is considerable asymmetry in U.S. and Soviet capabilities. American carrier-based fighters and fighter/bombers based in Europe could penetrate to the Soviet Union, and tactical missiles such as Pershings could reach Soviet allies.

The Soviets have some sea-based cruise missiles that possibly could be used to attack the United States, but the range of their MR/IRBMs and tactical missiles is restricted to Europe and China.

Because these issues are complicated and involve forces and concepts that are hard to isolate and define, the negotiations for follow-on agreements are likely to be long and arduous. They will be further complicated by the interrelationships between strategic and general purpose forces and by the difficulty of verifying qualitative restrictions as contrasted to simple limits on numbers of launchers.

The SALT II negotiations will also be affected by unilateral moves by either side to develop and deploy weapon systems within the limits of the present accords. Former Defense Secretary Laird and others have called for a vigorous weapon development program to ensure that the United States is not placed at a strategic disadvantage and to provide incentives for the Soviets to agree to more extensive controls.

A central theme in the administration's rationale for its strategic program has been the so-called bargaining chip approach. The Safeguard ABM system, for example, was long justified primarily as a means of encouraging the Soviets to agree to limit their deployment of offensive missiles, particularly the large SS-9s. After the signing of the SALT accords, Secretary Laird and U.S. military leaders argued that it was imperative to continue accelerated development of a new sea-based missile system (Trident) and a new bomber (B-1) if the Soviets were to agree to additional arms limitations.

At the same time some observers argued precisely the opposite—that it was American restraint in not matching the Soviets in numbers of launchers that prompted the latter to agree to the present accords. It was said that, given U.S. qualitative superiority and its advantage in strategic bombers, the Soviets would not have signed the agreements without the advantage in missile launchers on their side.

In its amendments to the resolution supporting the Interim Agreement and its approval of most of the Defense Department's request for strategic weapon modernization programs in fiscal 1973, the Congress has clearly supported the bargaining chip approach. Although this stance is not unalterable, it is likely to affect both unilateral American decisions regarding strategic forces and the U.S. bargaining position at Geneva.

Soviet Strategic Forces

American perceptions of Soviet actions and intentions are a major factor in U.S. strategic force planning. Estimates of the threat posed by Soviet nuclear weapons are used in evaluating U.S. strategies, missions, and weapon effectiveness. Force levels and qualitative standards are justified largely by their consequences for the U.S.–Soviet strategic balance. Moreover, changes in the Soviet force and U.S. reactions to them are judged to have profound political effects, both domestic and international.

It should be recognized that, while intelligence sources indicate quite accurately what the Soviets are doing today, any projection of their forces into the future becomes more uncertain with time. The Soviets themselves probably do not know what their strategic capabilities will be five years from now. That will depend not only on technical and economic developments in the Soviet Union, but on the actions other nations will take in the interim. Strategic planners thus are confronted with an uncertain game of action and reaction in which the United States and the USSR are the principals. The SALT agreements do, of course, lessen the uncertainties to a degree.

Since the early 1960s the United States has relied primarily on satellite reconnaissance to collect information on the deployment of Soviet strategic systems. The coverage and resolution (sharpness) of satellite cameras are sufficient to show clearly the physical characteristics of weapons that have been deployed and not effectively concealed, and the actual count of fixed sites such as missile silos and airfields.[17] Thus the United States has been able to discern new Soviet strategic systems soon after their appearance at test or operational sites and to estimate with reasonable precision the numbers of Soviet offensive and defensive missiles, of strategic submarines as they are launched, of radar sites, and of airfields. Since it is more difficult to take an accurate inventory of systems that are mobile and under cover during construction, some specialists are concerned about the U.S. ability to count systems such as mobile ICBMs.[18]

17. Resolution of the U.S. "Big Bird" satellite reportedly approaches 1 foot at an altitude of 100 miles, which is sufficient to distinguish a human being. Ted Greenwood, "Reconnaissance and Arms Control," *Scientific American*, Vol. 228 (February 1973), pp. 14–25.

18. Using ground-based radar and other surveillance systems, the United States has determined that the Soviet Union has a satellite reconnaissance program of comparable scope, though little is known of its quality.

For a detailed yet readable account of the U.S. satellite program from its inception, see Philip J. Klass, *Secret Sentries in Space* (Random House, 1971). Ted Greenwood, in Adelphi Paper No. 98 (London: IISS, 1972), relates the verification problems of arms control to the capabilities of reconnaissance and surveillance systems. Alec Galloway provides considerable technical data on the U.S. satellite program in "A Decade of U.S. Reconnaissance Satellites," *International Defense Review* (Geneva), Vol. 5 (English edition, June 1972), pp. 249–54.

Electronic and optical sensors, which are carried by aircraft and ships as well as by satellites, also furnish information on the performance of Soviet systems, particularly radars and missiles.

While these intelligence sources provide solid data on past Soviet deployments, they provide only indirect knowledge of Soviet strategy and plans for future deployments. Detection of a new system in its development phase gives no assurance that it actually will be deployed in significant numbers. However, once a deployment rate has been established by observation over time, it is possible to make deductions about production capacity.

The Soviet Union is known to have made a major buildup of its strategic forces since 1964. Table 2-1 shows the changes in Soviet strategic force levels, the major components of which are discussed below.

Land- and Sea-based Missiles

Between 1967 and 1971 the USSR added roughly 250 ICBM launchers to its operational inventory each year. Two-thirds of the force and the largest part of the buildup consists of SS-11 and SS-13 missiles, which can carry a payload in the 1 to 2 megaton range a distance of about 5,000 nautical miles.[19] The SS-13, which is the newer of the two, is a solid-fueled rocket similar to early versions of the U.S. Minuteman. Some 300 SS-9 missile launch sites, however, are what most concern U.S. planners. This giant weapon, first deployed in 1965, can carry a 20 to 25 megaton warhead some 6,500 nautical miles. It has also been tested with a multiple warhead—three each in the 4 to 5 megaton range—and with a modified payload for use as a fractional orbital bombardment system (FOBS).[20] Additionally, early in 1972 the United States identified almost 100 new silos under construction in the USSR that could be used either to launch a new missile, apparently even larger than the SS-9, or to provide SS-9 missiles with "harder" launch fa-

---

19. Unless otherwise noted, descriptions of Soviet weapon systems are taken from International Institute for Strategic Studies, *The Military Balance, 1972–1973* (London: IISS, 1972).

20. In such a system the missile would be propelled into an orbital trajectory but would be decelerated and reenter the earth's atmosphere before completing a full orbit. FOBS has the potential for reducing warning time, for attacks from unexpected angles, and for greater range, though at substantial cost to payload and accuracy.

Table 2-1. Soviet Strategic Force Levels at Mid-Year, Selected Years, 1964–73

Weapon system	1964	1968	1970	1973
Intercontinental ballistic missiles				
SS-7 and SS-8	200	220	220	220
SS-9	0	180	240	300
SS-11 and SS-13	0	400	840	1,070
Total	200	800	1,300	1,590
Submarine-launched ballistic missiles				
SS-N-4 and SS-N-5[a]	120	130	120	90
SS-N-6 and SS-N-8	0	0	160	530
Total	120	130	280	620
Heavy bombers				
Tu-95 (Bear)	120	110	100	100
Mya-4 (Bison)	40	40	40	40
Total	160	150	140	140
Defensive forces				
Antiballistic missile launchers	0	some	64	64
Surface-to-air missile launchers[b]	8,600	9,200	9,800	10,000
Fighter/interceptors[b]	4,000	3,700	3,300	2,900

Sources: Offensive missile and bomber totals for 1964–70 are from International Institute for Strategic Studies, *The Military Balance* (London: IISS, various years); totals for 1973 are from "United States Military Posture for Fiscal Year 1974," statement by Admiral Thomas H. Moorer before the Senate Armed Services Committee (March 28, 1973; processed). Distributions within totals are authors' estimates based on fragmentary data in various sources. Defensive forces are estimated from charts in *Fiscal Year 1973 Authorization for Military Procurement, Research and Development, Construction Authorization for the Safeguard ABM, and Active Duty and Selected Reserve Strengths*, Hearings before the Senate Armed Services Committee, 92 Cong. 2 sess. (1972), Pt. 2 (Authorizations), pp. 516 ff.; and "United States Military Posture for Fiscal Year 1974."

a. These totals include missiles aboard diesel powered submarines which, according to Admiral Moorer, are no longer considered "strategic missile forces in terms of the [SALT] Interim Agreement."

b. These numbers apparently reflect total Soviet air defense capabilities, including systems designed for tactical defense of Soviet ground forces. In 1972, Lieutenant General Otto J. Glasser, Air Force deputy chief of staff for research and development, gave the number of Soviet air defense systems "available for strategic air defense purposes" as 1,200 to 1,500 surface-to-air missiles and 1,800 to 2,300 interceptor aircraft. *Department of Defense Appropriations for Fiscal Year 1973*, Hearings before the Senate Appropriations Committee, 92 Cong. 2 sess. (1972), Pt. 4, p. 805.

cilities, thereby increasing their survivability.[21] Finally, not listed in the table are roughly 700 medium- and intermediate-range ballistic missiles deployed by the USSR whose range does not exceed 2,000 nautical miles.

The increase in submarine-launched missiles has been in the number of

21. Statement of Dr. John S. Foster, Jr., Director of Defense Research and Engineering, Department of Defense, in *Fiscal Year 1973 Authorization for Military Procurement, Research and Development, Construction Authorization for the Safeguard ABM, and Active Duty and Selected Reserve Strengths*, Hearings before the Senate Armed Services Committee, 92 Cong. 2 sess. (1972), Pt. 3, p. 1812.

SS-N-6 launchers, 16 of which are housed in each Yankee-class submarine. (In early 1972, the Soviets had 25 of these submarines in operation and 17 or 18 more under construction.) The missile can be launched under water and carries a warhead in the megaton range some 1,500 nautical miles. This weapon system is comparable to the early U.S. Polaris submarines carrying the A-1 missile. The Soviets have been testing a new submarine-launched missile, the SS-N-8, which will be of greater range, perhaps up to 4,000 miles. In 1972, press reports indicated that modified versions of Yankee-class submarines were being built (Delta class), each of which would carry 12 of these new missiles.[22] The older Soviet sea-based missiles, SS-N-4 and SS-N-5, are of very limited range (less than 700 nautical miles); they are deployed on a variety of submarines, both diesel and nuclear propelled. The SS-N-4 can be launched only from the surface.

Strategic Bombers

These are the weakest element in the Soviet strategic offensive force, consisting of fewer than 150 aircraft first built in the mid-1950s. Both the Tu-95 (Bear) and the Mya-4 (Bison) are subsonic, with an unrefueled range on the order of 6,000 nautical miles. Fifty more Bisons are configured as tankers. Their bomb loads are relatively limited (10 to 20 tons as against 30 to 35 tons for the U.S. B-52), but the Bears also carry one air-to-surface missile. The Soviets have developed prototypes of a new supersonic bomber, the Backfire, about whose potential strategic role U.S. defense officials appear uncertain in their public statements.

In addition to these strategic aircraft, the USSR has 700 medium-range bombers—the Tu-16 (Badger) and Tu-22 (Blinder)—which are not assigned to its strategic airforce.

Qualitative Factors

Simple numbers of missiles or aircraft are very poor indices of a nation's strategic capabilities. The actual performance of strategic forces in any given circumstance will depend on many qualitative factors—the weapons' reliability, the accuracy of delivery systems, the yield and composition of payloads, the survivability of launch platforms, the responsiveness of the command and control system, and so forth.

22. *Washington Post*, May 31, 1972; *New York Times*, October 1, 1972; *Aviation Week and Space Technology*, Vol. 97 (December 4, 1972), p. 5.

The Soviet Union traditionally has stressed the quantitative rather than qualitative aspects of military forces. Thus, while the Soviets have more than matched the United States in numbers of deployed missiles and have developed weapons with very large payloads, they are considerably behind the United States in many aspects of strategic weaponry.

It is precisely in this area that American knowledge of Soviet capabilities is most uncertain. Consequently, U.S. planners tend to assume the worst, attributing to the Soviets the best technical capability that the evidence allows; or, in the absence of empirical evidence, projecting U.S. technical capabilities onto the Soviets. This tendency can lead to expensive and unnecessary reactions to incorrect estimates based on limited information. On the other hand, to underestimate the threat could expose the United States to serious danger. Because of the long lead times of 5 to 10 years required to develop new strategic systems, this uncertainty has dictated a conservative approach in the past.

Most of the important debates concerning proposed new U.S. weapon systems focus on the quality of Soviet weapon performance. While a thorough discussion of these issues is precluded by their technical nature and by security restrictions, it is possible to highlight the relationship between several important qualitative factors and U.S. planning.

ICBM technology. Of greatest concern to the United States is the state of Soviet ICBM technology, in particular the attainment of higher accuracy and a capability to deploy multiple independently targetable reentry vehicles (MIRVs) on a single launcher. Once attained, these two capabilities, combined with the large number and large payload of Soviet land-based offensive missiles, could threaten the prelaunch survivability of U.S. land-based missile forces (see Appendix B).

Concern about a MIRV capability has arisen from Soviet testing of a triple warhead for the SS-9, a system that provides multiple warheads but not independently targetable ones. (Differences between reentry systems are discussed in Appendix A.) No tests have been reported since 1970, however, suggesting Soviet dissatisfaction with this system as a potential base for MIRV development. Additional concern stems from more recent Soviet tests of the SS-11, modified to improve its penetration capabilities, and with very recent tests of the SS-11 carrying a triple warhead.[23]

Official U.S. statements on Soviet MIRV technology have been rather

23. Statement of Dr. John S. Foster, Jr., p. 1812; *Washington Post*, Oct. 16, 1972. Note that an ability to disperse penetration aids is a far cry from mastery of MIRV technology.

ambiguous. For example, in announcing the most recent SS-11 tests, military spokesmen indicated that three warheads were associated with the reentry vehicle, but they were reticent about the critical issue of whether their impact points were sufficiently dispersed to indicate a true MIRV capability. In March 1973, Secretary of Defense Elliot L. Richardson noted that the USSR was developing three new, improved ICBMs, some with multiple reentry vehicles. He added, however, "We do not expect the Soviets to achieve the more sophisticated MIRV capability before the mid-1970s."[24]

The USSR is likely to try to deploy MIRVs, the important question being when it will succeed. U.S. intelligence once predicted that the USSR would have MIRVs as early as 1971. Secretary Laird indicated in 1972 that the USSR was only two years behind the United States in missile technology.[25] This assumption seems rather pessimistic; the United States successfully flight-tested its first true MIRV systems in August 1968, giving this country at least a five-year lead if the Soviet Union maintained the same rates of development and deployment. In operational terms, Dr. John S. Foster, Jr. stated in March 1972 that a middle estimate (neither optimistic nor pessimistic) would not give the Soviets enough missiles with MIRVs and the required accuracy to threaten Minuteman seriously before 1980.[26]

Estimates of Soviet missile technology have most directly affected past U.S. views on the advisability of deploying antiballistic missile defenses and taking other steps to improve the resistance of Minuteman launchers to nuclear attack. Given the limitation of ABMs in the SALT agreements, these estimates will now bear more directly on U.S. views on the advisability of shifting a greater part of the U.S. deterrent to sea-based systems.

Relative submarine survivability. This assessment depends on two independent factors: the "quietness" of strategic submarines, and the technology and size of antisubmarine warfare (ASW) forces. The United States now has a considerable lead in both factors, and U.S. strategic submarines are highly survivable, according to Secretary Laird and other officials.[27] No

24. "Statement of Secretary of Defense Elliot L. Richardson before the Senate Armed Services Committee on the FY 1974 Defense Budget and FY 1974–1978 Program" (March 28, 1973; processed), p. 32.

25. *Washington Post*, June 10, 1972.

26. Statement of Dr. John S. Foster, Jr., p. 1812.

27. See, for example, *Annual Defense Department Report, FY 1973*, pp. 41–42, and Statement by Admiral Elmo R. Zumwalt, Jr., in *Fiscal Year 1973 Authorization for Military Procurement . . . and Active Duty and Selected Reserve Strengths*, Senate Hearings, Pt. 3, p. 920.

similar public statements have been issued regarding the survivability of Soviet strategic submarines. The future is less certain, however. The Soviets are known to be devoting considerable effort to developing advanced acoustic technology for ASW, and concern about a possible breakthrough in this area influenced the U.S. decision to accelerate development of sea-based systems. A discussion of strategic ASW is included as Appendix C.

Defenses against strategic bombers. The Soviets conceivably could develop a number of technologies in various areas that could threaten the ability of U.S. strategic bombers to reach their targets. One would be the development of a capability to fire missiles, particularly those launched from submarines, on a depressed trajectory, thereby reducing the warning time available to bombers on the ground.[28] Another would be improvement in the capabilities of Soviet fighter/interceptor aircraft and surface-to-air missiles to engage U.S. bombers at low altitudes. The United States is taking several measures to counter these possibilities, including the dispersal of bombers to a greater number of air bases, the deployment of a short-range attack missile (SRAM), and development of a subsonic cruise armed decoy (SCAD). Both of the latter systems will improve the chances that U.S. bomber forces could penetrate to and destroy their targets (see Appendix D).

The Strategic Balance

As has been noted, the basic objective of U.S. strategic forces is to deter an attack on this nation by being able to absorb an opponent's first strike and to destroy in retaliation a large part of the aggressor's industry and population. The capability of U.S. forces to attain this objective can be measured only in a complex dynamic model of nuclear exchange. No static comparison of U.S. and Soviet strategic forces, no matter what index is employed, is an adequate measure of the retaliatory capabilities of the two nations. Both the United States and the Soviet Union are generally recognized already to have deployed enough retaliatory forces to meet this objective many times over. Interest in static comparisons persists nonetheless, as was shown in the debate over ratification of the SALT agreements in the U.S. Senate in the summer of 1972. This interest is based on the political consequences imputed to quantitative force level imbalances.

28. In the employment of a depressed trajectory, the path of the missile is deliberately lowered so as to shorten flight time and to delay detection by ground-based radars.

Table 2-2 shows the U.S.–USSR strategic balance in mid-1972 and projects that balance to mid-1977 under two alternative conditions. The first 1977 projection shows the balance that could have been expected had the SALT agreements not been attained, assuming that Soviet deployments continued at rates previously noted and that the United States completed the strategic programs then under way. The second projection assumes that each side modernizes its forces only within the limits of the agreements. The year 1977 was chosen for the comparison because it is the terminal date of the Interim Agreement limiting offensive weapons. Additionally it is a

Table 2-2. Strategic Forces of the United States and the Soviet Union, 1972 and Projected to 1977, with and without the Strategic Arms Limitation Agreements[a]

| | 1972, operational or under construction | | 1977 | | | |
| | | | United States | | USSR | |
Forces	United States	USSR	Programmed	Under SALT	Potential without SALT	Under SALT
Limited by agreements						
ICBMs	1,054	1,618	1,054	1,000	2,250	1,410
SLBMs	656	650–740[b]	656	710	1,050	950
Total	1,710	2,268–2,358	1,710	1,710	3,300	2,360
Not limited by agreements						
Heavy bombers	457	140	448	448	130	130
Total offensive forces	2,167	2,408–2,498	2,158	2,158	3,430	2,490
Independent warheads (operational)						
Missile	3,428	1,970	5,890	6,320	6,500[c]	3,700[c]
Heavy bomber	2,460	250	3,800	3,800	250	250
Total	5,888	2,220	9,690	10,120	6,750	3,950
Antiballistic missiles (operational)						
Launchers	0	64	302	200	1,000	200

Source: Adapted from data supplied to the Senate Foreign Relations Committee in a National Security Council study dated June 1972. *Congressional Record*, daily ed., Aug. 3, 1972, p. S12603. The following notes were appended by the committee.

a. In compilations, it is useful to compare equivalent megatonnage—a measure of the destruction capacity of an arsenal in light of various components and weapons sizes. The committee has not yet succeeded in obtaining from the executive branch unclassified numerical comparisons. The Defense Department informs the committee, however, that, in terms of equivalent megatonnage, the Soviet Union has "about the same as" the United States. The situation in 1977 is expected to be similar.

b. The smaller number reflects the U.S. estimate of the number of launchers on integral submarine hulls under construction on May 26, 1972. From the Soviet viewpoint, more submarine hulls for SLBMs could not be considered as "under construction" because major subsystems are being built for hulls not yet being assembled on integral units. The number 740 was negotiated as a firm baseline which circumvents the difficulty in defining the construction process.

c. Soviets do not yet have MIRVs. Soviet warhead totals for 1977 represent rough estimates of possible totals. Potential Soviet missile warhead total based on reasonable assumptions of intensive effort by Soviets. Soviet missile warhead total represents our best judgment of what Soviets might do under SALT. Assumption of all-out MIRV conversion effort by Soviets could add 1,500 to 1,900 more warheads to Soviet SALT total by 1977 but only at expense of placing many heavy missile forces under conversion and hence out of operation during some of period of agreement. This is considered highly unlikely. Moreover, the United States could also increase force loadings on programmed delivery systems in face of such maximum effort.

point in time when U.S. programs currently in the procurement stage will be completed, but before next-generation systems, such as the Trident system or B-1 bomber, could begin to be deployed.

Table 2-2 indicates that the SALT agreements give the USSR an advantage in numbers of missile launchers—some 2,360 compared to 1,710 for the United States. *It is important to realize, however, that if the momentum of the Soviet buildup were not halted by the agreements, the USSR could by 1977 have almost twice as many missiles as the United States, assuming that its strategic deployment program continued as before.* To counter this buildup the United States could have launched an urgent building program of its own, turning out additional Minuteman missiles, for example; but to have done so would have entailed major expenditures and yielded no assurance of greater security.

Furthermore, U.S. technological advantages and its lead in strategic bombers combine to present a more favorable balance in other, more significant measures of strategic capabilities. In 1972 the United States held more than a two-to-one lead in numbers of strategic warheads. This margin is likely to increase by 1977; by then the United States will have completed its two MIRV programs (Minuteman III and Poseidon), but the Soviets will be unlikely to have deployed substantial numbers of MIRVed missiles.

Unfortunately the data in the table provide no comparison of the two forces in equivalent megatonnage. This measurement—which takes account of the number of warheads in the strategic force, their yield, and the fact that their destructive potential is theoretically proportional to the two-thirds power of the yield—is perhaps the best single index of nuclear deterrent capability. Footnote *a* to the table indicates that the U.S. and Soviet strategic forces are likely to have "about the same" equivalent megatonnage in both 1972 and 1977. Our own calculations agree with this assessment, indicating that approximate parity will exist in the range of 4,000 to 4,500 equivalent megatons. As a benchmark, it may be noted that 400 equivalent megatons delivered against the opposing targets are usually considered more than enough to destroy a large part (at least 25 percent) of either the American or the Soviet population.[29]

29. The 400 equivalent megaton figure refers to deliverable megatonnage. The 4,000–4,500 figure is not strictly comparable because it includes weapons on nonalert aircraft, on submarines not on patrol, on unreliable missiles, and so on. Even cutting the projected figures in half, however, would provide a more than adequate margin of urban/industrial destruction.

The Chinese Nuclear Force

Since the explosion of their first nuclear device in 1964, the Chinese have made considerable progress toward the development of operational strategic nuclear weapons. Although the Chinese nuclear force will present only limited threats to this nation through the end of the decade, U.S. military planning will have to take Chinese capabilities increasingly into account.

China's Weapon Systems

At the end of 1972 the Chinese presented a limited nuclear threat in Asia. According to the International Institute for Strategic Studies, they may have produced enough fissionable material for a total of 150 fission and fusion weapons.[30] The main vehicles for delivery of these weapons are some 200 IL-28 (Beagle) Soviet-built light bombers—20-year-old planes that can carry only one small weapon less than 800 nautical miles. They are slow and easily defeated by modern air defense fighters or surface-to-air missiles.

This force will probably decline in size as China builds and deploys its own version of the Soviet-designed Tu-16 (Badger) medium bomber. This aircraft is reportedly in serial production at a rate of about four or five a month; it can carry three or four low yield weapons, or perhaps two 3-megaton weapons, up to 1,600 nautical miles.[31] The Tu-16 force, which could number 150 aircraft in 1974, potentially threatens several major Soviet cities as well as targets in Japan, Korea, Taiwan, India, and the Philippines. Additionally, though they are obsolescent by Western standards, the Tu-16s would have a higher probability of penetrating air defense systems than would the IL-28s, particularly if they used low altitude tactics.

The Chinese are also pursuing a cautious but steady ballistic missile development program. Admiral Thomas H. Moorer, chairman of the Joint Chiefs of Staff, testified in 1973 that they have had a medium range missile (MRBM—600 to 1,000 nautical miles) for many years and that it probably is now operationally deployed.[32] The International Institute for Strategic

---

30. *The Military Balance, 1972–1973.*
31. *Washington Post*, September 18, 1970; *Annual Defense Department Report, FY 1973.*
32. "United States Military Posture for Fiscal Year 1974," Statement by Admiral Thomas H. Moorer before the Senate Armed Services Committee (March 28, 1973; processed), p. 26.

Studies reports that 20 to 30 MRBMs have been deployed and are operational.[33] Secretary Laird reportedly predicted in 1970 that the Chinese would have 80 to 100 MRBMs by the mid-1970s, each with a warhead of 20 kilotons.[34]

The deployment of MRBMs has lagged behind Western predictions for several years, perhaps because China also is developing an intermediate range ballistic missile (IRBM—1,500 to 2,500 nautical miles). In early 1972, U.S. sources reported that a "handful" of these missiles had been deployed. Each new missile is said to carry a 3 megaton warhead. Subsequently, "administration officials" were quoted as saying that the Chinese had deployed a limited number of a third type of missile with a range of about 3,500 miles. The same source gave 20 as the number of deployed MRBMs and earlier IRBMs.[35] There is no firm basis for predicting either the rate of IRBM production or the eventual mix of medium and intermediate range weapons.

Aside from range advantages that would expose Moscow and other cities in western Russia to Chinese nuclear attack for the first time, the new IRBMs would be less vulnerable than earlier Chinese weapons. They are said to use a storable liquid propellant, permitting them to be installed in underground silos. The MRBMs, being liquid fueled at time of launch, have to be kept above ground and are slow to launch and difficult to hold in an alert status. Additionally, the IRBMs' extended range could be used to deploy these weapons away from China's borders, making them less vulnerable to conventional ground or air attack.

None of these weapons threatens the United States directly. To attain that capability, the Chinese would have to overcome several technological obstacles in order to (1) improve their missiles' accuracy, (2) ensure that their limited number of weapons are survivable enough not to become potential targets for a U.S. first strike, and (3) attain the range and payload capabilities required by the extremely long distance between China and the United States. The third factor is particularly important: urban areas in the eastern United States are about 6,000 nautical miles from Chinese territory, and the closest continental U.S. targets are about 4,200 nautical miles dis-

33. *The Military Balance, 1972–1973.*
34. *Northern Virginia Sun* (Arlington), December 14, 1970.
35. Reports of the IRBM deployment appeared in *New York Times*, February 1, 1972. Admiral Moorer's statement, cited in note 32 above, was made later and was less definitive regarding the deployment. The most recent report referred to above appeared in *New York Times*, November 8, 1972.

tant. China's problem is complicated by the fact that its ICBMs would have to overfly the USSR in order to strike most targets in the United States.

Any intercontinental threat posed by China to the United States would originate in land-based missiles. Secretary Laird reported in 1972 that the Chinese do not have and are not developing long-range bombers.[36] They do have one G-class diesel powered ballistic missile submarine, but have no missiles for it. They are also known to be building a nuclear powered submarine, probably of the attack variety. In short, there is no evidence to suggest that Chinese SLBMs will pose a threat during the 1970s. Any early version of a Chinese nuclear submarine would probably be very noisy and hence vulnerable to U.S. antisubmarine warfare forces.

While the Chinese have not yet flight-tested an ICBM, they could do so in the near future.[37] U.S. defense officials have projected a Chinese force of 10 to 20 ICBMs by mid-1976,[38] but this forecast appears less and less plausible. Given the extremely tight limits on Chinese resources (estimates of Chinese defense expenditures range from $8 billion to $16 billion a year), China may defer ICBM deployment for the indefinite future. Such a decision would be based on the assumption that the Soviet Union is a much greater threat to Chinese security than is the United States. Under such an assessment the Chinese presumably would use their resources to develop regional nuclear capabilities and conventional defenses against Soviet attacks rather than build a few relatively vulnerable missiles capable of striking the United States. While one should expect the Chinese to continue their ICBM development program as a hedge against a renewal of U.S.–Chinese tension, a deployment decision before the end of the decade is not at all inevitable.[39]

Potential Impact on U.S. Planning

The development of Chinese nuclear forces has affected past U.S. decisions regarding the deployment of antiballistic missile and aircraft defense

36. *Annual Defense Department Report, FY 1973*, p. 45.

37. One missile test was said possibly to have been a reduced-range test of a missile with intercontinental potentiality. A more plausible interpretation is that the device being tested was the 3,500-mile-range missile referred to previously.

38. *Annual Defense Department Report, FY 1973*, p. 45; "United States Military Posture for Fiscal Year 1974," p. 26.

39. This view is given added weight by reports stressing China's emphasis on tactical nuclear weapons. See, for example, Joseph R. L. Sterne, "Chinese Pepper in the SALT," *Baltimore Sun*, October 6, 1972. For a contrasting view, see *New York Times*, March 4, 1973.

systems. The Sentinel ABM proposed by the Johnson administration was justified almost entirely as a light area defense system capable only of protecting the United States from the limited kind of threat that China could mount. While the Safeguard ABM proposed by the Nixon administration in 1969 was primarily justified as a means of ensuring the survivability of Minuteman against expected developments in Soviet missile forces, its potential for expansion into a more capable area defense system than Sentinel was an important factor in the executive decision to aim for a twelve-site system. Similarly, defense against potential Chinese attacks was sometimes cited in arguments for modernizing U.S. defenses against aircraft.

The common thread running through these views was a fear that deterrence, as it was believed to operate against the USSR, would not be effective against China. It was thought that China, because a relatively small part of its population lives in cities[40] and because of certain values ascribed to its leaders, would not necessarily be deterred by U.S. maintenance of a secure retaliatory capability. Thus, it was argued, once the Chinese gained the ability to strike the United States, it would be necessary to obtain a U.S. first strike capability against their strategic forces and to protect the U.S. civilian population from attack. Later these arguments were refined to an extent. It was said that such steps were necessary to make American defense commitments in Asia credible—that the Chinese would not believe the United States would risk Seattle in order to defend Tokyo. In either case the essence of the argument was the same: that Chinese leaders' values were somehow different from those of Russian leaders, consequently that China would not be subject to the same restraints.

American acceptance of the ABM limitations in the SALT accords indicates rejection of these arguments. The limits on deployment of ABM launchers and radars apply to any system, whatever its target. Additionally the agreement prohibits the deployment of ABM systems outside the nation's borders, ruling out various systems that, because of their design and location, could be directed only against the Chinese.[41] Clearly, then, the United States will have to depend on the maintenance of a secure retaliatory capability to deter China no less than the USSR.

40. The 200 largest Chinese cities contain only 9 percent of the Chinese population but 80 to 90 percent of the industrial capacity. *Fiscal 1973 Authorization for Military Procurement . . . and Active Duty and Selected Reserve Strengths*, Senate Hearings, Pt. 3, p. 1872.

41. For example, a Navy proposal (SABMIS) envisaged a ship-launched ABM that would intercept offensive missiles before they entered the terminal part of their trajectory.

This is not so difficult as it might seem, despite the rural nature of Chinese society. Although it would be impossible to hold a large part of China's total population as hostage, China's industry and technically proficient population are concentrated in its large cities. About 200 equivalent megatons delivered on target would destroy from 80 to 90 percent of China's industry and 10 percent of its population, or some 75 million people—certainly sufficient hostage to deter any but insane leaders.

Since 200 equivalent megatons represents less than 5 percent of present and projected U.S. forces, the Chinese urban/industrial target structure places no significant incremental requirements on U.S. force level planning. In fact, considerable reductions in U.S. strategic force levels could be made, perhaps as the result of SALT II agreements, without affecting American ability to deter China for the foreseeable future.

The Chinese nuclear force nonetheless may affect the U.S. force mix. Given the unsophisticated nature of Chinese air defenses, bombers are probably the weapon best suited for a possible U.S.–Chinese conflict. They could penetrate and recover through Chinese defenses with impunity, leaving U.S. missile forces intact for continued deterrence of the USSR. Should it be deemed necessary to buy incremental missile forces for anti-Chinese missions—for example, as the result of a decision to obtain a first strike capability—sea-based systems would be preferable, since they would not have to overfly the Soviet Union. Two to four submarines carrying MIRVed missiles should be sufficient for the counterforce task.

China is likely to loom large in Soviet strategic planning, for Chinese deployments to date, as well as China's verbal accounts of its nuclear strategy, seem to be directed primarily at the USSR. The Soviets' perceptions of their requirements regarding China may affect their force structure and their willingness to agree to further limits on strategic armaments. The Soviets already have redeployed some air defense and MR/IRBM forces from western Russia to central Asia in response to the growing Chinese nuclear capability. The importance the USSR attaches to China's nuclear forces was made clear when, at the height of the 1969 Sino-Soviet border dispute, the Soviets reportedly threatened through third parties to destroy Chinese nuclear facilities.

While the requirements posed by China may make the Soviets reluctant to discuss some topics suggested by the United States in SALT II—for example, limiting MR/IRBMs—agreements could be designed to take account of these problems—for example, by limiting only mobile MR/IRBMs and weapons deployed at fixed sites in western Russia. Furthermore, as was the case for the United States, the requirements posed by the Chinese target structure should place only modest incremental needs, if any, on Soviet force levels; they would not justify substantial force allocations.

CHAPTER THREE

ISSUES AND ALTERNATIVES

As the preceding chapter suggested, each strategic weapon system is part of a larger defense posture that is shaped by numerous forces, political and economic as well as military. Within this overall posture, the evolution of U.S. strategic missile programs will be a central national security issue over the next several years:

• Missiles are generally considered to be the cornerstone of the U.S. nuclear deterrent.

• The cost of developing and procuring the Trident missile and submarines to carry them probably will be the largest ever associated with a single weapon system. Ten submarines equipped with missiles are expected to cost at least $13.5 billion dollars.[1]

• The Interim Agreement limiting strategic offensive missiles is more controversial than the ABM Treaty, since it allows the Soviet Union about 50 percent more missiles than the United States. On the other hand, the United States now has a substantial technological lead. The question of what steps should be taken to maintain that lead is a pressing issue that increasingly will become the focal point of debate over strategic forces.

• The concept of transferring U.S. missiles from land to sea challenges the existing allocation of missions and resources among the military services.

Interest in the bomber force will probably focus on the high cost of procuring the B-1. Moreover, the day-to-day costs of operating existing bombers and tankers are high relative to those of other components of the Triad,

---

1. *Report on Authorizing Appropriations for Fiscal Year 1973 for Military Procurement, Research and Development, Construction, Authorization for the Safeguard ABM, and Active Duty and Selected Reserve Strengths, and for Other Purposes*, S. Rept. 92-692, 92 Cong. 2 sess. (1972), p. 29. This cost estimate is very conservative and may already be out of date in 1973.

34

principally because of the large number of people needed to support the bomber force. Significant reductions in operating costs could be made, of course, by cutting the number of operational aircraft.

The SALT agreements have settled the question whether to deploy a large ABM force, at least for the time being, but an issue of secondary concern remains: the utility of continued investment in research and development to protect the Minuteman ICBMs with ABMs.

For air defenses, the primary issue is the extent to which they could be reduced and tailored to more limited strategic defense objectives consistent with the SALT agreement and U.S. strategic doctrine.

The following sections discuss the currently planned programs for each of the strategic components and project the resulting force structures and costs over the next several years. In addition they describe alternative programs and indicate their costs and effectiveness. A more detailed discussion of effectiveness and operational factors is provided in Appendixes A through D; Appendix E outlines the methods used to develop cost data throughout the study.

Land-based Missiles

Land-based ICBMs pose difficult issues for U.S. planners, since they are the part of the Triad considered most likely to become vulnerable to a Soviet attack. To lessen that risk, a series of survivability measures have been undertaken in recent years, the most expensive and best publicized of which is the Safeguard program. Less public attention has been paid to the current program to modernize the Minuteman force by MIRVing the missiles and improving their launch silos, even though these steps have cost nearly $1 billion a year in the past and will continue to require substantial expenditures through fiscal 1979. Modernization consists of replacing older Minuteman missiles with Minuteman III, each capable of carrying three independently targetable reentry vehicles. The new missile costs about $4.5 million, exclusive of the Atomic Energy Commission's expenditures for nuclear materials.[2] In addition the older missile silos must be modified, at a

2. *Fiscal Year 1972 Authorization for Military Procurement, Research and Development, Construction and Real Estate Acquisition for the Safeguard ABM and Reserve Strengths,* Hearings before the Senate Committee on Armed Services, 92 Cong. 1 sess. (1971), Pt. 2, p. 1301.

cost of almost $800,000 each, so that they can accept the MIRVed Minuteman III.[3]

Another modernization measure is the development of Command Data Buffer, a computer capability to be added to the Minuteman command and control system. Command Data Buffer will enable missile commanders to change targets for each missile much more rapidly, greatly increasing the number of targets against which each missile can be directed. The Air Force has estimated that total acquisition costs for this system will be $286 million.[4]

The Air Force is also undertaking the Silo Upgrade program, to reduce missile silos' vulnerability to nuclear effects by modifying equipment within the silo. Costs of these changes, such as improving the missile suspension system and power supplies, will total more than $1.0 billion from fiscal 1973 through 1977.[5]

The Air Force strategic missile program for fiscal 1973 through 1980 is outlined in Table 3-1, together with its costs. These estimates are based on the assumption that the administration plans to convert Minuteman II as well as Minuteman I missiles to the MIRVed Minuteman III, hence that all 1,000 Minuteman missiles will have multiple independently targetable warheads. Previously, only 550 Minuteman I missiles were to have been MIRVed, but the 1974 budget request includes $23 million to procure long lead-time items needed if the remaining single-warhead Minutemen are also to be replaced. Although the Air Force had long favored this course of action, it was accepted only recently by the Defense Department. The decision probably reflects two goals: to increase the residual capacity of that part of the Minuteman force that survived a Soviet first strike, thus prolonging the period during which Minuteman would be a credible part of the Triad; and to contribute to maintaining American superiority in numbers of warheads if the Soviet Union should MIRV its own missiles.[6]

Funds for converting the 550 Minuteman I missiles—about $6 billion—will have been almost completely appropriated by the end of fiscal 1974.

3. *Ibid.*, p. 1317.

4. *Department of Defense Appropriations for 1972*, Hearings before a Subcommittee of the House Committee on Appropriations, 92 Cong. 1 sess. (1971), Pt. 5, p. 1139.

5. *Ibid.*, p. 1137.

6. *Fiscal Year 1973 Authorization for Military Procurement, Research and Development, Construction Authorization for the Safeguard ABM, and Active Duty and Selected Reserve Strengths*, Hearings before the Senate Committee on Armed Services, 92 Cong. 2 sess. (1972), Pt. 2, pp. 1165–66.

Table 3-1. Projected Numbers and Costs of Air Force Strategic Missiles, Fiscal Years 1973–80

Category	1973	1974	1975	1976	1977	1978	1979	1980
Missiles deployed at end of fiscal year								
Minuteman I	190	90	0	0	0	0	0	0
Minuteman II	500	500	450	330	210	90	0	0
Minuteman III	310	410	550	670	790	910	1,000	1,000
Titan II	54	54	54	54	54	54	54	54
Costs by fiscal year (total obligational authority in millions of constant fiscal 1974 dollars)								
Major system acquisition	830	780	680	640	580	540	340	140
Other investment costs	1,360	1,520	1,250	870	730	660	460	260
Direct operating costs	370	370	360	360	360	360	360	360
Indirect operating costs	400	410	390	390	390	390	390	390
Total	2,960	3,080	2,680	2,260	2,060	1,950	1,550	1,150

Source: Authors' estimates based on data in various Defense Department publications and in hearings on the fiscal 1972 and 1973 Defense Department budgets before the Senate and House Armed Services and Appropriations Committees. See App. E for a description of the makeup and derivation of each cost category.

The additional cost of MIRVing the 450 Minuteman II missiles will be about $1.9 billion—roughly $400 million a year from fiscal 1975 through 1978 and $300 million in fiscal 1979. These costs would rise if the production lines were closed and had to be reopened to pursue this option later in the decade.[7]

Alternatives for Minuteman

The central problem facing the Minuteman force is its potential vulnerability, an issue discussed in detail in Appendix B. The MIRV program alleviates the problem by increasing the number of warheads that would survive a first strike, but this benefit could be negated by further improvements in Soviet missiles. Hence the MIRV program provides only a temporary solution.

If land-based missiles are to remain a viable part of the Triad beyond the mid-1980s, the United States might consider two courses of action. One is to defend its land-based missiles with ABMs. Such deployments are limited, however, by the ABM Treaty, and in any case they could be overwhelmed by counterdeployments of additional Soviet offensive weapons. The ad-

7. *Military Implications of the Treaty on the Limitation of Anti-Ballistic Missile Systems and the Interim Agreement on Limitation of Strategic Offensive Arms*, Hearing before the Senate Committee on Armed Services, 92 Cong. 2 sess. (1972), p. 429.

ministration nevertheless hopes to preserve this option by investing heavily in ABM research and development.

A second possible option is to make future generations of land-based missiles mobile, thus making it more difficult to target them successfully. The fiscal 1974 budget request includes data suggesting that such a course is being considered and, in fact, the first evidence of a possible follow-on to Minuteman: $6 million is requested to begin developing the subsystem technologies that would be needed for mobile ICBMs. While the present request is small, it is potentially very significant. If it were decided to proceed with full development and acquisition of mobile ICBMs, the program would make a major impact on the budget in the 1980s.

An alternative course would be to reduce reliance on land-based missiles, perhaps by moving away from the Triad toward a two-component strategic force. Such a course would rest on the assumption that any measure to improve Minuteman's prelaunch survivability or the destructive potential of surviving missiles could be negated by the Soviet Union at relatively lower costs. The USSR could do so by deploying additional warheads on its own missiles or by improving their accuracy or yield. Holders of this view consider any further investment in land-based missiles to be shortsighted. More importantly, they consider the existence of a vulnerable component of the strategic force to be destabilizing to U.S.–Soviet relations in that, in time of extreme crisis, the Soviet Union might be tempted to strike first so as to reduce the damage it could expect to receive from a U.S. strike.

Two programs for reducing dependence on land-based missiles could be considered. Either would be implemented on the assumption that the weapons being phased out would be replaced by sea-based missiles when the new Trident submarine becomes available in the 1980s. Such a shift would require adjustments in the Interim Agreement on offensive weapons, but the present accord expires in 1977 in any event.

One program would emphasize the desirability of moving gradually, to minimize the political consequences of force level reductions. It would be assumed that the Soviet Union would not acquire a sufficient MIRV capability to threaten a first strike against Minuteman before the 1980s, hence that land-based missiles would retain some utility through the end of this decade. The option would end new investment in land-based missiles with the completion of the MIRV program for Minuteman I. At its peak, therefore, the Minuteman force would consist of 550 MIRVed Minuteman III and 450 single warhead Minuteman II missiles. The program then would gradually eliminate all land-based missiles by 1985. Roughly 100 missiles would be removed each year, with Minuteman III squadrons the last to go. This program would save an average of approximately $600 million a year, compared to our projection of the administration's program for fiscal 1974 through 1980.

The second possible program would eliminate Minuteman more quickly, reflecting a less optimistic view of Soviet MIRV capabilities or a heavy discounting of the political consequences said to follow unilateral force reductions. The program would halt all investment in land-based missiles immediately and phase out Minuteman within a few years. It would save about $1.5 billion annually from fiscal 1974 through 1980, compared to our projection of the administration's program for this period. Additional savings could be obtained from the Safeguard ABM program at the same time, since there would be no reason to continue Safeguard deployments or operations if Minuteman were removed from the force.

A choice between the administration's program and either of these alternatives would depend primarily on an assessment of Soviet MIRV capabilities and the effect of Minuteman vulnerability on the stability of U.S.–Soviet relations. Those that are less concerned by the potentially destabilizing effects of Minuteman vulnerability point out that the possible savings are not large; Minuteman operating costs are much lower than those of sea-based missiles or bombers. It is argued that Minuteman, even if vulnerable, is useful in providing a flexible response in limited war, in forcing the Soviets to program a large part of their ICBMs for attacking Minuteman, and in confronting them with the problem of launching simultaneous and coordinated attacks on both missile sites and bomber bases.

The Future of Titan

The Titan II missile is the largest U.S. ballistic missile, carrying a warhead with an estimated yield of 5 to 10 megatons.[8] It is also the oldest missile in the U.S. inventory; however, since it uses a storable liquid propellant, aging is not as severe a problem as it is with solid propellant missiles such as Minuteman and Polaris. Current costs of the Titan force arise almost exclusively from operations, maintenance, and indirect support. While these

8. International Institute for Strategic Studies, *The Military Balance, 1972–1973* (London: IISS, 1972), p. 65.

expenses are much larger per missile than those of Minuteman, the total cost is only about $50 million a year.

The Interim Agreement provides for replacement of the 54 Titan II missiles by a like number of sea-based missiles. A decision to do so would hinge on an assessment of the value of maintaining these few large warheads in the U.S. missile force and of their usefulness in future SALT negotiations. In any event, Titan II is likely to be replaced once the new Trident submarines become available in the 1980s.

Sea-based Missiles

The sea-based missile force is an essential part of the U.S. strategic deterrent. Because the mobility and concealment of the submarine platforms currently assure invulnerability of the system, sea-based missiles offer better prospects for high rates of survivability than either land-based missiles or bombers, now and for the foreseeable future (see Appendix C).

When conversion of the 31 Polaris submarines to carry Poseidon missiles is completed in 1976, the United States will have more than 5,000 warheads deployed on submarine-launched missiles. (Each Poseidon can carry up to 14 small yield MIRV warheads, estimated at 50 kilotons by the International Institute for Strategic Studies.) Taking on-station status and missile reliability into account would leave at least half of these warheads, or about 2,500, for delivery on Soviet targets. The redundancy supplied by the bombers and land-based ICBMs can be viewed as adding to confidence in the deterrent capability of the Polaris/Poseidon force—a capability that is substantial now and will continue to be so for the next several years.

Acceleration of Trident

In 1972 the administration recommended and the Congress approved a dramatic increase in the pace of spending for a follow-on sea-based system, now called Trident. Under this program a new missile, Trident I, with a longer range of about 4,000 nautical miles, will be developed for possible use in both Polaris/Poseidon and Trident submarines by 1978. Trident II, a missile with the extended range of an ICBM (about 6,000 nautical miles), will also be developed for possible deployment in the early 1980s. The first Trident submarine could be operational by 1978, two or three years sooner than previously planned.

Table 3-2. Projected Numbers and Costs of Naval Strategic Forces, Fiscal Years 1973–80

Category	1973	1974	1975	1976	1977	1978	1979	1980
Missiles deployed at end of fiscal year								
Polaris	432	336	240	160	160	160	144	80
Poseidon	224	320	416	496	496	496	496	496
Trident	0	0	0	0	0	0	24	96
Costs by fiscal year (total obligational authority in millions of constant fiscal 1974 dollars)								
Major system acquisition	1,530	2,200	2,800	3,100	3,000	2,800	2,900	2,900
Other investment costs	1,330	1,240	1,170	1,240	1,330	1,550	1,570	1,620
Direct operating costs	520	520	520	520	520	540	560	580
Indirect operating costs	760	700	700	700	700	720	740	760
Total	4,140	4,660	5,190	5,560	5,550	5,610	5,770	5,860

Source: Same as for Table 3-1.

Table 3-2 projects the accelerated deployment schedule for Polaris, Poseidon, and Trident missiles through fiscal 1980, with a conservative estimate of the associated costs. The most striking aspects of these projections are that:

• The decision to accelerate Trident was made when the Navy was midway in the conversion of Polaris missiles to Poseidon missiles—a conversion justified as a hedge against an extreme ABM threat that has not materialized.

• Costs of the fleet ballistic missile program increased in fiscal 1973 and are continuing to grow dramatically because of the cost of Trident research, development, and procurement, and the cost of completing the Poseidon conversion program.

• Indirect costs are a substantial part of the costs of the sea-based missile program. They result from the large establishment ashore that is required to support the Polaris force.

It has always been clear that a follow-on to the Polaris/Poseidon force would ultimately be required, if for no other reason than that the Polaris submarines are aging; the oldest will have been in service about 20 years in 1980. It has been generally accepted that Trident should be this replacement. An important issue, however, concerns the timing of replacement, or the necessity for the fiscal 1973 acceleration in the Trident development program. It is useful to review the rationale that led to acceleration:

• The ten oldest Polaris submarines needed to be replaced.

• The longer-range missile would allow operation from bases in the United States without sacrificing on-station time.

• There was a need to hedge against possible improvements in Soviet antisubmarine capabilities, primarily by increasing the potential operating area of U.S. submarines, a benefit associated with the longer-range missile (see Appendix C).

• Trident would provide a bargaining chip for the next phase of SALT.

• The capability of U.S. land-based ICBMs would have to be transferred to sea at some future time.

The urgency that would justify an acceleration of the operational date of Trident by two to three years cannot be attached to the first three reasons. The older Polaris submarines will not become obsolete within that short time span; the present Polaris Atlantic fleet could be based in the United States at only a small sacrifice of on-station time; and the antisubmarine warfare (ASW) threat, to the extent one exists, would be greatly alleviated by the new longer-range missile that would have been available at the same time under the old program.

Thus the last two reasons provide the main arguments for the acceleration of Trident: to encourage the Soviets in arms negotiations, and to provide more sea-based missiles to relieve concern for the survivability of Minuteman in the late 1970s. Judgments made regarding these arguments will largely determine whether the accelerated pace of Trident development will be maintained. Some have contended that these arguments do not warrant increased spending in the near term, furthermore that continuing an accelerated schedule increases the likelihood of growth in the real cost of these systems. It is argued that the concurrency of development and procurement necessitated by the accelerated schedule, and the need to proceed with hastily drawn and poorly defined contracts, may lead to real cost growth of major proportions. In fact, there have been some indications that the $13.5 billion total program cost estimate already may be in error.

The following are conservative estimates of comparative major system acquisition costs of the accelerated Trident program, with an initial operational capability in about 1978, and the previous slower program, with an initial operational capability in 1981 (costs represent total obligational authority in millions of constant 1974 dollars):[9]

	Fiscal years						
	1974	*1975*	*1976*	*1977*	*1978*	*1979*	*1980*
Accelerated program	1,700	2,500	3,100	3,000	2,800	2,900	2,900
Slower program	700	900	1,000	1,500	2,000	2,700	2,800

9. Derived by authors on the assumption that the total Trident purchase will exceed the presently planned 10 submarines.

Submarine-launched Cruise Missiles

A second issue concerning U.S. sea-based strategic missiles was raised after the SALT agreements, when Secretary Laird recommended development of a submarine-launched cruise (air-breathing) missile as a potential addition to U.S. strategic offensive forces. In fiscal 1973, $4 million was obligated for development of this system; $15 million is requested in fiscal 1974. Detailed technical characteristics and costs of the system have not been revealed; it is known, however, that a cruise missile based on the Harpoon (a tactical missile under development by the Navy) could be launched from a submerged submarine. The range, payload, type of navigation system, and number of missiles aboard each submarine are important measures of its potential effectiveness that are not yet available to the public.

The new system is recommended as an additional bargaining chip to induce the Soviets to agree to restrictions on their own force of cruise missile submarines in SALT II.[10] A submarine-launched cruise missile could also provide benefits in penetrating Soviet defenses, should the USSR abrogate or violate the ABM Treaty and develop major missile defenses.

Opposition to the new system is based on two arguments. First, it is said that the benefits to be derived from the program are not clear, or at least that the incremental capabilities the new weapon would provide are uncertain, given the ABM Treaty and the penetration capability of already deployed U.S. systems, particularly the air-to-surface missiles carried by bombers. Second, it is argued that the Soviet reaction to such an undertaking is unpredictable. The USSR might, it is said, view the program as a means for the United States to circumvent the spirit if not the letter of the SALT agreements, and consequently be less willing to reach further agreements.

The Bomber and Tanker Force

Of the six strategic components, the bomber force is the most expensive to maintain. If the new B-1 bomber is ordered into production in the mid-

10. The United States developed a submarine-launched cruise missile (Regulus) in the later 1950s, but this force was disbanded early in the 1960s under Secretary of Defense McNamara. The USSR has some 60 cruise missile–equipped submarines; however, they are of limited range, appear to be designed for antiship operations, and thus are usually considered tactical naval weapons. See R. T. Pretty and D. H. R. Archer (eds.), *Jane's Weapon Systems, 1971–72* (London: Jane's Yearbooks, 1971), pp. 43–47.

seventies, the acquisition cost of aircraft alone would probably exceed $10 billion dollars, three-fourths as much as the ten-ship Trident program. Over the next few years, critics are certain to ask whether these high costs could be justified by the B-1's contribution to the U.S. deterrent.

Current Programs

Bombers were the mainstay of U.S. strategic forces from the end of the Second World War until ballistic missiles became available in large numbers in the mid-sixties. From a peak of more than 1,600 aircraft in the late 1950s, the size of the force has declined to less than 500 today. Marked reductions were made early in Secretary McNamara's tenure, when almost 1,000 B-47s were phased out. During the Nixon administration, all of the B-58s and many of the older model B-52s also have been eliminated from the active force. The decline in numbers is not, however, reflected in a like decrease in capability. The bombers (predominantly B-52s) in the present force are larger, are better equipped with avionics and electronic countermeasures, and have a longer range than the bombers of the 1961 force, which consisted mostly of B-47s. Moreover, the introduction of more efficient fusion weapons has increased the destructive power in the payload of the current force.

From the congressional testimony of senior Air Force officials it is possible to deduce a fairly complete picture of Air Force planning for bombers and for the air-to-surface missiles they carry. One such interpretation is shown in Table 3-3, which estimates bomber force levels for fiscal 1973 through 1980 and their costs.

Several points call for elaboration.

Each B-52 currently can carry two Hound Dog air-to-surface missiles as well as decoys, called Quail, that simulate the bomber to enemy radars. The Hound Dog and Quail are derived from relatively old technologies and are inferior in performance to the new short-range attack missile (SRAM), now entering the force, and to the subsonic cruise armed decoy (SCAD) being developed by the Air Force.

An often overlooked but significant supporting element is the tanker force, which refuels bombers in the air en route to their targets. Note that Table 3-3 shows more tankers than bombers in the projected force. Each strategic bomber requires about one tanker, the difference being accounted for by the requirement for tankers to support tactical fighters as well.

Table 3-3. Projected Numbers and Costs of Air Force Bombers, Air-to-Surface Missiles, and Tankers, Fiscal Years 1973–80

Category	1973	1974	1975	1976	1977	1978	1979	1980
Aircraft and missiles deployed at end of fiscal year[a]								
B-52D–F[b]	142	117	117	117	117	117	87	57
B-52G–H[b]	255	255	255	255	255	255	255	255
FB-111	66	66	66	66	66	66	66	66
B-1	0	0	0	0	0	0	30	60
Tankers[b]	615	615	615	615	615	615	615	615
Air-to-surface missiles								
Hound Dog, SRAM, SCAD	350	540	740	940	1,150	1,140	1,200	1,300
Costs by fiscal year (total obligational authority in millions of constant fiscal 1974 dollars)								
Major system acquisition	750	680	770	1,600	2,100	2,300	2,500	2,600
Other investment costs	1,230	1,340	1,410	1,840	1,930	2,110	2,240	2,300
Direct operating costs[b]	1,570	1,530	1,470	1,470	1,470	1,470	1,470	1,470
Indirect operating costs[b]	2,020	2,070	1,980	1,980	1,980	1,980	1,980	1,980
Total[b]	5,570	5,620	5,630	6,890	7,480	7,860	8,190	8,350

Source: Same as for Table 3-1.

a. Number of aircraft deployed in operational squadrons. The total inventory contains a greater number of aircraft of each type, the balance being procured to compensate for attrition, and for other purposes.

b. Although the B-52s and tankers operating in Southeast Asia are not on day-to-day alert as part of the strategic force, their costs continue to be borne in the strategic budget. The table reflects all but the incremental costs imposed by the war in Southeast Asia.

Total costs of the Air Force bomber program are estimated to be about $6 billion to $8 billion a year from fiscal 1974 through 1980. About half this amount—some $3.5 billion a year—consists of direct and indirect operating costs. For a squadron of fifteen bombers, *direct* operating costs of about $30 million a year are accounted for by personnel pay and the costs of fuel, replacement parts, a share of base flight operations, and a share of intelligence and communications. A squadron's *indirect* operating costs, estimated to be about $40 million a year, include maintenance of central depots for aircraft and engine overhaul, shared costs of base support facilities such as hospitals, training of aircrews and maintenance personnel, and part of the costs of higher headquarters. Perhaps one-third of the indirect costs are fixed and would not vary over the near term with small changes in the size of the bomber force, but others, such as training costs, will vary with force size. The operating costs of a tanker squadron are about two-thirds those of a bomber squadron.

Major system acquisition costs are relatively small in comparison to these operating and other acquisition costs. Even the acquisition costs (R&D and procurement) of the relatively expensive B-1 aircraft would probably not exceed $2 billion annually, and the cost of procuring SCAD and SRAM will not exceed $0.5 billion a year.

Table 3-4. Allocation of the Strategic Force Budget by Component, Fiscal Year 1974

Total obligational authority in billions of dollars

Category	Cost	Percent of total
Offensive systems		
Land-based strategic missiles	3.1	*17*
Sea-based strategic missiles	4.7	*26*
Bombers	5.6	*31*
Subtotal	13.4	*74*
Defensive systems		
Ballistic missile defense	1.3	*7*
Air defense	3.2	*18*
Civil defense	0.1	*1*
Subtotal	4.6	*26*
Total	18.0	*100*

Source: Estimated from data in Department of Defense, "Program Acquisition Costs by Weapon System" (processed; disseminated with Defense Department News Release 44-73, Jan. 29, 1973) and in various authorization and appropriation hearings in the House and Senate on the Defense Department budget for fiscal 1973. Indirect costs are allocated among weapon systems in proportion to direct operating costs (see App. E for cost definitions). Incremental costs of the war in Southeast Asia are excluded.

To provide a broader perspective, Table 3-4 compares the costs of the bombers with those of the other components of the U.S. strategic force in fiscal 1974. The bomber program is by far the most expensive element, accounting for more than 30 percent of total strategic costs on an annual basis, or three-fourths as much as the Minuteman and Polaris/Poseidon forces combined. As the following sections indicate, several issues bear on the future costs of strategic bombers.

Could Bomber Force Levels Be Reduced without Greatly Sacrificing Capability?

In connection with its fiscal 1974 budget proposals, the administration announced its intent to phase out two squadrons of older model B-52s. Although seventeen B-52s had been shot down over Southeast Asia in late 1972, the Defense Department said that its plan reflected only "fact-of-life retirements of B-52Ds that have reached the end of their structural life."[11]

If one sought further reductions in direct and indirect operating costs—the major contributors to total costs of the bomber program—the most

11. Defense Department News Release 44-73, January 29, 1973.

feasible approach would be to eliminate the remaining older model B-52Ds and the FB-111s, which are the least effective aircraft in the force. Under present plans the approximately 100 operational B-52Ds will be used primarily to carry gravity bombs; they are not scheduled to be modified to carry either SRAMs or SCADs. Without these new air-to-surface missile systems, the B-52Ds will add little to the penetration capability of the bomber force. The FB-111 is severely limited in both range and payload, and its supersonic capability is not important for penetration of Soviet air defenses. (The Air Force already has phased out the B-58 bomber, an aircraft whose performance was comparable to that of the FB-111.) Any reductions in the bomber force would allow comparable reductions in the tanker force, since each bomber requires approximately one tanker for refueling.

What would be the capability of the residual force if these reductions occurred? The alert force of approximately 100 B-52G–H models can be expected to survive any Soviet preemptive strike, provided currently planned survival measures are completed. This alert force will carry a payload of about 600 equivalent megatons of nuclear weapons consisting of gravity bombs, SRAMs, and SCADs. Even if only one-third of these weapons were delivered, the alert bomber force alone would have the capability to destroy more than 10 percent of the Soviet population and 50 percent of Soviet industry. A follow-on bomber would add to this capability as it became operational.

The essential questions concerning the present force are twofold: Is addition of the marginal capability of the B-52Ds and FB-111s to an already substantial capability worth its cost of $8 billion to $10 billion over the next seven years?[12] Will maintenance of these marginal forces encourage the Soviets to reach a SALT II agreement on offensive weapons?

Characteristics of the Follow-on Bomber

If the United States is to maintain strategic bombers as an element of its deterrent, it will have to introduce a follow-on aircraft in the 1980s. What should be its characteristics?

12. In 1972 the administration withdrew all of the older B-52s and about 50 of the new models from the day-to-day alert force and deployed them to Southeast Asia, showing tacit recognition that these approximately 180 bombers are not essential for deterrence.

The B-1 currently is the only candidate. As now conceived, it would offer marginal improvements over the B-52G–H models in speed, low altitude capability, radar cross-section, payload, and prelaunch survivability (engine start time, airframe vulnerability to nuclear blast, and flyout speed after takeoff). The range of the B-1 would be comparable and in some cases somewhat superior to that of the B-52G–H models for similar payloads and flight profiles. It is not clear that these marginal improvements, either singly or in combination, would reduce dependence of the bomber force on SCAD to assure penetration of advanced Soviet area air defenses. Other factors affecting bomber penetration are discussed in Appendix D.

Criticism of the B-1 has centered on its high cost. Estimates of unit acquisition costs range from $45 million to $90 million (including a proportional share of research and development, initial spares, and so on); operating costs for each bomber and its supporting tanker would be about $10 million a year.[13] But the B-1 program now has so much momentum in the executive branch and opposition in the Congress is so diffuse that the research and development program probably will be authorized in its entirety. However, during the mid-1970s, when a procurement decision is to be made, many present concerns about its cost and performance may be found to be justified. A point may be reached where a new bomber is deemed essential, yet there will be no feasible alternative to the B-1.

An alternative approach would be to undertake the parallel development of a manned bomber designed solely to carry standoff cruise missiles, like the Air Force SCAD but with a nuclear warhead, which could penetrate at very low altitude and present a very small radar target. Thus it would not depend on decoys to penetrate Soviet interceptor defenses. Because this bomber would not be required to fly as far or at as low an altitude as penetrating bombers, and because it would be able to carry more fuel than the B-1, it would not require tankers for refueling. Since it would not need to penetrate Soviet air defenses, it could be large and subsonic, like a Boeing 747 or Lockheed C-5. And it could incorporate the same improvements in ground alert and takeoff capability as the B-1.

Another alternative would be to develop the cruise missile for the B-1, a course that would offer collateral advantages:

13. In 1972 testimony before the Senate Armed Services Committee, General Ryan gave unit flyaway costs as $30 million and unit program acquisition costs as $45.5 million. *Military Implications of the Treaty . . . on Limitation of Strategic Offensive Arms*, Senate Hearing, p. 481.

Table 3-5. Costs of the B-1 and of a Standoff Bomber, Fiscal Years 1974–83ᵃ
Billions of fiscal 1974 dollars

Item of expense	240 B-1s	120 standoff bombers
Research, development, testing, and evaluation	1.5	1.0
Procurement[b]	16.6	10.2
Operating[c]	6.3	3.6
Total	24.4	14.8

Source: Authors' estimates.

a. Assumes that each standoff bomber could carry three times as many standoff missiles as could the B-1 but would not deliver gravity bombs.

b. Assumes average unit procurement cost of $65 million for 240 B-1 aircraft including avionics, $65 million unit cost for 120 standoff aircraft, and $0.5 million for each air-to-surface missile.

c. Includes cost of the supporting tanker force.

- The missile could be used on the B-52s as well, enabling them to avoid the need to penetrate Soviet air defenses at low altitudes. This would extend the B-52s' service life, allowing postponement of the decision to procure either the B-1 or a standoff bomber.
- Possibly a cruise missile could be launched from existing tankers (KC-135s), thus diversifying the uses of those aircraft.

Research and development costs for the standoff bomber should be relatively low, since the system would be based on aircraft and missile systems now in operation or under design. Because the standoff bomber would carry many more air-to-surface missiles than the B-1, not as many aircraft would be required. The smaller force and the absence of tankers could result in substantial savings in procurement and operating costs. The first ten-year costs of a force of 240 B-1s and of a comparable force of 120 standoff bombers are shown in Table 3-5.

In summary, this alternative has the potential to provide at least as much capability as the B-1 program at lower cost. Savings would result from reductions in total procurement, in long-term operating costs, and in the present tanker force. The standoff bomber would also avoid substantial costs by eliminating the need for a new tanker. Congressional testimony by the commander in chief of the Strategic Air Command suggests that a new tanker to support the B-1 will be an urgent requirement later in the 1970s.[14]

Evaluation of the standoff bomber alternative is subject to certain tech-

14. *Fiscal Year 1972 Authorization for Military Procurement . . . and Reserve Strengths*, Senate Hearings, Pt. 2, p. 1690.

nical and operational uncertainties. The first relates to the reliability and accuracy of the navigation system for the standoff air-to-surface missile. The second concerns the ability of the standoff missile to penetrate advanced defenses at the target: the Air Force does not believe that SCAD could penetrate an advanced terminal surface-to-air missile system effectively.[15] The third concerns the possible vulnerability of a standoff bomber to Soviet defensive systems that might operate several hundred miles from the Soviet homeland. However, there are no indications that such a threat will emerge, and substantial obstacles make its emergence unlikely. An investment now in relevant research and development should make it possible to resolve these uncertainties in time to make an informed choice between the standoff and penetrating (B-1) bomber within several years.

Ballistic Missile Defenses

Whether to build antiballistic missile (ABM) systems, for years the most contentious issue in the U.S. defense budget, has been made largely hypothetical by the SALT agreements. The administration apparently has decided for the time being not even to build the ABM site at Washington, D.C., allowed by the ABM Treaty. The Congress rejected a 1972 request for funds to plan the site, and no money for this purpose was requested in the administration's budget proposals for fiscal 1974. A remaining question, however, is the level of ABM research and development that should be maintained, within the limits of the agreement, as a hedge against possible Soviet violation or abrogation of the SALT accords.

Savings under the ABM Treaty

In the absence of a SALT agreement, and assuming congressional authorization, the Defense Department had planned to procure the twelve-site Safeguard ABM system and to strengthen an unspecified number of sites with new "Site Defense" radar and advanced interceptor missiles. Safeguard was intended primarily to defend Minuteman installations against a preemptive attack by Soviet missiles. The first site was to become operational by fiscal 1975; at the rates of funding evident between fiscal 1969 and

15. *Ibid.*, Pt. 4, p. 3120.

1972, the last would have been completed in fiscal 1986. Site Defense was to become operational in the very late 1970s.

From fiscal 1968 through 1972, some $5 billion was authorized for Safeguard. The fiscal 1973 budget proposal, issued long before the SALT accords were attained, included $1.5 billion to complete the first two Safeguard sites, to continue work on the third and fourth sites, and for advanced planning on the fifth. The budget also included $100 million for continued development of Site Defense. In total, the direct cost of ballistic missile defenses would have averaged $1.6 billion a year through the end of the decade.[16]

As a result of the SALT agreements, plans for U.S. ABM deployments were curtailed drastically. As was noted, the ABM Treaty permits each signatory to build only two operational ABM sites—one at an offensive missile installation and one in defense of the National Command Authority (NCA). Each site is further restricted in numbers of interceptor missile launchers, radars, and so forth. Consequently, plans for the twelve-site Safeguard system were canceled; construction was halted at the second site (Malmstrom Air Force Base), and advanced planning was terminated at the third and fourth sites. The Defense Department proposed to continue planning for the NCA site at Washington, as permitted by the agreement,[17] but the Congress declined to authorize the $29 million requested for this purpose.

These steps reduced the fiscal 1973 appropriations for missile defenses by some $650 million. Over the rest of the decade the reductions should save roughly $1 billion a year from the $1.6 billion annual expense cited above. Part of this amount, however, will be used to hedge against uncertainties regarding the future of the ABM Treaty and continued Soviet adherence to it.

How Much to Spend for Hedges?

In his testimony to the Congress on the SALT accords, Secretary Laird emphasized the need for the United States to maintain a vigorous research and development program in ballistic missile defenses and offensive tech-

---

16. This figure does not include indirect support costs or research and development not directly related to Safeguard or Site Defense.

17. Statement of Secretary of Defense Melvin R. Laird, *Strategic Arms Limitation Agreements*, Hearings before the Senate Foreign Relations Committee, 92 Cong. 2 sess. (1972), p. 63.

nology as a hedge against possible violation or abrogation of the agreements. At that time, the Defense Department requested a $110 million supplemental appropriation to provide for (1) an increase in spending for Site Defense, (2) an acceleration of the submarine-launched cruise missile research program, (3) an increase in the Advanced Ballistic Reentry Systems (ABRES) program to develop improved reentry vehicles, and (4) improvements in military command, control, and communications.

Evidently the Congress disagreed with the administration's assessment of the need for these incremental programs; substantial cuts were made in the first two elements of the request, and the third—the ABRES increase— was dropped altogether.[18] Nonetheless, the question of the degree to which research should be accelerated to hedge against future uncertainties regarding the ABM Treaty remains an important one.

The administration has requested nearly $500 million for ABM research and development in fiscal 1974—$217 million for Safeguard, $170 million for Site Defense of Minuteman, and about $100 million for research on advanced ballistic missile defenses. Some observers consider these amounts excessive in view of the ABM Treaty. The amount requested for Safeguard development seems particularly high, inasmuch as construction of that system is essentially complete.

Air Defense

After a major expansion in the second half of the 1950s, U.S. air defenses have become smaller since 1962. Army spokesmen have estimated that the direct cost of continental air defense declined from $1.8 billion in fiscal 1963 to $1.2 billion in fiscal 1972—a decrease of roughly 67 percent in constant dollars. This reduction can be attributed mainly to the Soviet Union's failure to develop a large force of strategic bombers; such a buildup was foreseen in the 1950s and led to accelerated deployments of early warning systems, manned interceptors, and defensive missiles. Currently, however, the Soviet strategic bomber force is quite small, consisting of only

18. *Authorizing Appropriations for Fiscal Year 1973 for Military Procurement, Research, and Development, and for Anti-Ballistic Missile Construction; and Prescribing Active Duty and Reserve Strengths*, H. Rpt. 92-1388, 92 Cong. 2 sess. (1972), pp. 18–19. See also *Department of Defense Appropriation Bill, 1973*, H. Rpt. 92-1389, 92 Cong. 2 sess. (1972), pp. 211–12.

about 100 Tu-95 (Bear) aircraft and 40 Mya-4 (Bison), both of which were in production in the mid-1950s.

In his Defense Report for fiscal 1973, Secretary Laird stated four objectives for the U.S. air defense system: (1) to deter air attacks by defending strategic offensive forces and important urban/industrial targets, (2) to defend the National Command Authority, (3) to limit damage from small air attacks, and (4) to prevent unauthorized overflights in U.S. airspace. He noted further that existing air defense weapons, sensors, and control mechanisms were inadequate to this task. Specifically, he mentioned the vulnerability of the command and control system, the inability of warning systems to detect aircraft penetrating at low altitudes, and the lack of a "look down, shoot down" capability against low-flying bombers. (See Appendix D for further discussion.) Accordingly, in the words of Secretary Laird, the administration decided "to make some selected reductions in the current force levels, accepting some additional risks in the near term *while pursuing development of more effective air defense components for the future.*"[19]

Attainment of more effective air defenses would require large expenditures. As described by Defense Department officials, the necessary modernization programs—including an improved manned interceptor (IMI), a new surface-to-air missile (SAM-D), an airborne warning and control system (AWACS), and a new type of over-the-horizon radar (OTH-B)—probably would entail more than $5 billion in acquisition costs alone. Nearly $300 million was authorized for development of these systems in fiscal 1972. In the following year the administration requested more than twice this amount, including funds for the procurement of three test aircraft for AWACS. The Congress, however, decided to retain AWACS in research and development, and made substantial cuts in the overall program.[20]

More recently the administration seems to have rethought the role of strategic air defense and to have modified the objectives of continental air defenses considerably. A 1973 Defense Department publication describes strategic air defense forces as being "capable of defending against a small bomber attack with a few days warning such as might occur in a crisis. This

---

19. *Annual Defense Department Report, FY 1973*, Statement of Secretary of Defense Melvin R. Laird before the Senate Armed Services Committee on the FY 1973 Defense Budget and FY 1973–1977 Program (February 15, 1972), pp. 66 and 73. (Italics added.)

20. H. Rpts. 92-1388 and 92-1389; Department of Defense, "Program Acquisition Costs by Weapon System" (processed; disseminated with Defense Department News Release 44-73, January 29, 1973).

force will have the inherent capability to restrict the unauthorized penetration of U.S. airspace."[21] Thus the first and second objectives stated by Secretary Laird would no longer seem to be significant in structuring U.S. air defenses.

The reasons for this reduction in air defense goals are probably threefold:

First, there is still little evidence that either major potential adversary of the United States is developing a long-range bomber force. As was noted previously, the Soviet Union's force of long-range bombers is small and has not been expanded since the mid-1950s. While the USSR has developed and already deployed prototypes of a new twin-engined, swing-wing bomber (Backfire), reports indicate that this aircraft has a less than intercontinental range. Thus it is probably intended as a follow-on to the Soviet Union's force of medium-range bombers, which, in the event of war, would be used against targets in Europe or China and against U.S. naval task forces at sea. While medium-range aircraft possibly could reach targets in the northern United States on one-way missions or if accompanied by tanker aircraft, the failure of the Soviet Union to develop new long-range bombers and tankers indicates that it does not now consider the long-range bomber mission important. Similarly, China currently has no aircraft capable of reaching the United States (without several refuelings), nor is there evidence that China is developing such weapons.[22]

Second, and more important, attainment of the ABM Treaty limiting the deployment of ballistic missile defenses has strengthened arguments against active air defenses. Since the United States has publicly and explicitly accepted its continued vulnerability to Soviet missile attack, why, critics ask, should it expend large sums to defend against a Soviet bomber force that presents, in equivalent megatonnage, only one-ninth to one-third the threat posed by the Soviet missile force? It has been estimated that even if the United States built an *impenetrable* bomber defense, the Soviets could compensate for the resulting reduction of their destructive potential by increasing the equivalent megatonnage of their missile forces by 11 to 33 percent.[23] Proponents of this view argue that since the United States depends

21. Department of Defense, "Military Manpower Requirements Report for FY 1974" (February 1973; processed). See also *Washington Post*, January 28, 1972.

22. *The Military Balance, 1972–1973; Evening Star & Daily News* (Washington), October 12, 1972.

23. Statement by Dr. Jeremy J. Stone, *Fiscal Year 1972 Authorization for Military Procurement . . . and Reserve Strengths*, Senate Hearings, Pt. 5, p. 3746.

on the logic of deterrence to prevent missile attacks on its territory, and since a missile attack would be far more destructive than existing bomber threats, there is no reason why deterrence should not prevail against bomber threats as well.

Finally, the administration's decision may have been prompted, in part, by the hostility toward strategic air defense modernization evident in the Congress. This attitude was reflected, for example, in the cuts made in the fiscal 1973 request for air defense modernization.[24]

Whatever the reasons for the decision, curtailment of strategic air defense objectives could have significant budgetary consequences. In 1972 we projected the average annual cost of strategic air defense at $4.8 billion (in fiscal 1974 dollars) for fiscal 1973 through 1979.[25] Our present estimate for fiscal 1974 through 1980 averages $4.3 billion a year, a saving of $500 million annually. This projection is detailed in Table 3-6. Within the Defense Department, debate continues as to the precise force levels and modernization schedules necessary to attain even the modest new objectives for strategic air defense. Decisions on some specific issues, discussed below, could result in additional savings of up to $900 million a year.

Interceptors

At the end of fiscal 1973, the United States maintained seven manned interceptor squadrons equipped with F-106 aircraft in the active Air Force and sixteen Air National Guard squadrons equipped with F-101s, F-102s, and F-106s. These force levels are somewhat smaller than those maintained in fiscal 1968 and roughly one-third the size of those maintained in 1962. The present force embodies some qualitative improvements, however.

The Defense Department has indicated that it is considering plans to acquire an improved manned interceptor (IMI) for strategic defense later in the decade, as a replacement for existing aircraft. Earlier plans for procurement of an aircraft especially designed for this purpose have been dropped, and a modification of the F-14, F-15, or possibly the F-4 will be used instead. The F-15 would be the likeliest choice, since both it and the IMI

---

24. Also see *Fiscal Year 1972 Authorization for Military Procurement . . . and Reserve Strengths*, Senate Hearings, Pt. 5, and *Fiscal Year 1973 Authorization for Military Procurement . . . and Selected Reserve Strengths*, Senate Hearings, Pt. 6.

25. Charles L. Schultze and others, *Setting National Priorities: The 1973 Budget* (Brookings Institution, 1972), pp. 102–04.

Table 3-6. Projected Size and Costs of Strategic Air Defense, Warning, and Control Forces, Fiscal Years 1973–80

Category	1973	1974	1975	1976	1977	1978	1979	1980
Interceptor squadrons								
Active Air Force	7	7	7	7	7	7	7	7
Air National Guard	20	20	20	20	20	20	20	20
Surface-to-air missile batteries								
Active Army	21	21	21	21	21	21	21	21
National Guard	27	27	27	27	27	27	27	27
Airborne warning and control squadrons								
EC-121	2	2	2	2	1	0	0	0
AWACS	0	0	0	0	1	2	4	4
Costs by fiscal year (total obligational authority in millions of constant fiscal 1974 dollars)								
Major system acquisition[a]	320	290	500	800	1,200	1,200	1,500	1,500
Other investment costs	570	570	940	980	1,100	1,150	1,200	1,200
Direct operating costs	1,130	1,140	1,100	1,100	1,100	1,100	1,100	1,100
Indirect operating costs	1,220	1,240	1,200	1,200	1,200	1,200	1,200	1,200
Total	3,240	3,240	3,740	4,080	4,600	4,650	5,000	5,000

Sources: Authors' estimates based on data in *Fiscal Year 1972 Authorization for Military Procurement, Research and Development, Construction and Real Estate Acquisition for the Safeguard ABM and Reserve Strengths,* Hearings before the Senate Armed Services Committee, 92 Cong. 1 sess. (1971), Pt. 2; *Fiscal Year 1973 Authorization for Military Procurement, Research and Development, Construction Authorization for the Safeguard ABM, and Active Duty and Selected Reserve Strengths,* Hearings before the Senate Armed Services Committee, 92 Cong. 2 sess. (1972), Pt. 6; Department of Defense, "Program Acquisition Costs by Weapon System" (processed; disseminated with Defense Department News Release 44-73, Jan. 29, 1973); Department of Defense, "Military Manpower Requirements Report for FY 1974" (February 1973; processed); and other hearings before Senate and House committees. See App. E for a description of the makeup and derivation of each cost category.

a. The new surface-to-air missile (SAM-D), the improved manned interceptor (IMI), and the airborne warning and control system (AWACS) may be used for both strategic air defense and general purpose forces. Consequently some of their costs are shared. Research and development costs of the first two systems are carried in the general purpose force budget and not included in these figures. On the other hand, all AWACS research and development costs are borne by the strategic budget and included here. Procurement funds have been allocated between the two budget accounts in proportion to the number of systems planned to be procured for each, as indicated in congressional testimony in 1971 and 1972.

would be Air Force managed programs. Use of an existing aircraft design bears the advantage of saving research and development costs—a factor that is keeping current strategic defense budgets relatively low. At a unit cost of approximately $8 million, the projected purchase of seven IMI squadrons (194 aircraft) would total slightly more than $1.5 billion.

Given the reduced scope of strategic air defense, procurement of the IMI could be justified solely as an economic replacement for existing interceptor aircraft that have reached the end of their useful lives. The timing of replacement would depend on a technical assessment of the capabilities of existing aircraft and the cost and effectiveness of possible successors. The F-106 primary interceptors were first delivered to the Air Defense Command in 1959, and all were operational in 1960. If their replacement could be delayed until the 1980s, projected strategic air defense costs could be reduced by an average of some $200 million a year from fiscal 1974 through

1980. More broadly, consideration could be given to reducing present interceptor force levels in line with the reduction in strategic air defense objectives. A program to phase out seven squadrons over two to three years would yield additional annual savings of $150 million during fiscal 1974–80.

Surface-to-Air Missiles

At the end of fiscal 1973, the United States maintained 21 Nike-Hercules missile batteries in the active Army and 27 Nike-Hercules batteries manned by National Guardsmen for strategic air defense. In addition, there were 4 Nike-Hercules batteries in Florida and 3 in Alaska, plus 8 Hawk batteries in Florida that were not part of the Army Air Defense Command and not considered strategic forces. These force levels may be contrasted to the more than 200 Ajax and Nike-Hercules batteries maintained in 1961.

Until 1973, the Army intended to replace all Nike-Hercules units with a new surface-to-air missile, SAM-D, for strategic defense. Plans called for the procurement of 84 SAM-D firing units; at an estimated unit cost of $20 million, the total cost would have been almost $1.7 billion. Moreover, there were signs that these cost projections would rise sharply.[26]

With the retrenchment in strategic air defense objectives, these plans no longer seem pertinent. SAM-D is no longer referred to in the context of strategic air defense, but is now said only to "provide Air Defense for ground troops."[27] Further, the restatement of air defense objectives implies that the readiness of surface-to-air missile forces will be lowered, since warning will be required before the system could defend against even small bomber attacks. This suggests that National Guard batteries will not be manned full time, as they were in the past.

These retrenchments, in particular the decision not to procure a follow-on surface-to-air missile, raise doubts about the need to maintain existing batteries for strategic air defense. A program to phase out these forces would save an average of $250 million a year from fiscal 1974 through 1980. On the other hand, if the decision on SAM-D were reversed and the system acquired for strategic defense, air defense costs would increase by an average of $200 million to $300 million a year.[28]

26. *Washington Post*, June 10, 1972.

27. "Program Acquisition Costs by Weapon System," p. 35.

28. In his fiscal 1974 budget presentation, Secretary of Defense Richardson noted SAM-D's possible use in a strategic role. "Statement of Secretary of Defense Elliot L. Richardson before the Senate Armed Services Committee on the FY 1974 Defense Budget and the FY 1974–1978 Program" (March 28, 1973; processed), p. 61.

Warning and Control Forces

Little or no public debate arises from Defense Department plans regarding most of these forces. Facilities in this category include various satellite systems, the North American Air Defense Command (NORAD) and regional control centers, the ballistic missile early warning system (BMEWS), over-the-horizon radar systems (OTH-A and B), Spacetrack (a system to detect and observe objects in space), and the SLBM (submarine-launched ballistic missile) detection and warning system. However, controversy does exist regarding the advisability of developing the airborne warning and control system (AWACS), an advanced electronic system to provide mobile warning and intercept control capabilities. Decisions on AWACS in turn will determine what is done with older radars and control systems, including the distant early warning (DEW) line and the semi-automatic ground environment (SAGE).

Under the previous air defense modernization plan, some 42 AWACS were to have been acquired by fiscal 1979. Twenty-nine of these were to have been used for strategic defense and the remainder for tactical missions. As AWACS became operational, older radar and control systems were to have been phased out. Discontinuance of DEW line operations was to have been delayed somewhat, however, since radar coverage in the northern sector depends on overcoming technical difficulties in the north-looking OTH-B site.

Under the reduced objectives for strategic air defense, these plans will draw renewed criticism, though procurement of a smaller number of AWACS might still be justified strictly as an economic replacement for ground radars and control systems. Cutting proposed AWACS procurement in half and delaying it a few years could save nearly $300 million a year from fiscal 1974 through 1980.

CHAPTER FOUR

THE STRATEGIC POSTURE IN AGGREGATE

The U.S. strategic posture—the image of strategic nuclear power that the United States projects to the world—emerges from resolution of the issues discussed in the preceding pages and of many others. The issues are resolved inductively through decisions reached by many persons in various organizations, each decision being made relatively independently. In theory, however, one can also consider alternative strategic postures in the aggregate, by making a number of simplifying assumptions and by focusing on the three major dimensions of strategic planning: *doctrine*—defining the purposes of nuclear weapons, how they would be used (if at all), and the degree of confidence required in planning for various contingencies; *military needs*—the kinds and quantities of weapons required and the rate at which they should be developed, procured, and retired in order to meet the objectives of strategic doctrine; and *political needs*—determining the kinds and quantities of weapons and development programs considered necessary to fulfill the nation's foreign policy goals.

In this chapter we project the aggregate strategic posture that will result if present Defense Department plans are carried forward through 1974–80. We then describe alternative postures based on different assumptions as to doctrine, military needs, and political requirements, and the tradeoffs between costs and imputed effectiveness.

The Present Strategic Program

Arguing that substantial efforts are necessary to meet the requirements posed by the doctrine of strategic sufficiency and emphasizing the political consequences of force level imbalances, Defense Department officials have asserted the need to maintain the Triad and to modernize each of its ele-

59

ments at a rapid pace. The main features of the resulting program are (1) an accelerated schedule for developing the Trident submarine and longer-range submarine-launched missiles, (2) a continued moderate development schedule for the B-1 bomber, (3) completion of the MIRV program for the Poseidon and Minuteman missiles and the deployment of short-range attack missiles (SRAM) in the bomber force, and (4) completion of a one-site Safeguard ABM system. Additionally, some modernization programs for air defenses will be carried out during the decade. In general, missiles will be maintained at their present levels and replacements phased in on a one-for-one basis; the older bombers, however, may be phased out without replacement.

The average annual cost of this program, in constant 1974 dollars, is estimated to be $20.2 billion during fiscal 1974 through 1980. This figure and all subsequent total force cost estimates include indirect support costs (for example, the cost of training and medical care for strategic manpower), civil defense expenses (assumed to be fixed at $90 million a year), and a proportionate share of defense agency costs. These figures exclude the cost of warhead development and procurement, which is usually borne by the Atomic Energy Commission (AEC) and not publicly announced.[1] They also exclude the incremental costs imposed on the strategic bomber force by military operations in Southeast Asia.

In considering possible alternatives to this program, several constraints should be borne in mind.

First, any alternative must use the existing force as a starting point. Except for reductions in existing force levels, several years are needed to make significant changes in force structures or weapon development programs. Consequently the fiscal and military effects of even radical departures are unlikely to be realized for a long time. The political effects of announced changes, however, can be almost immediate.

Second, there is a link between strategic and conventional general purpose forces. If the total defense budget is fixed, an increase in spending for general purpose forces will result in reduced expenditures for strategic weapons. Conversely, any reduction in conventional capabilities probably will result in increased reliance on nuclear forces to deter war. Consequently, any analysis (including this one) that omits general purpose forces must be considered incomplete.

1. The AEC's total annual expenditures for military purposes probably do not exceed $1.5 billion, including costs associated with tactical weapons.

Third, the qualitative characteristics of weapon systems are closely related to the effectiveness of the total force. In the case of strategic weapons, qualitative differences can be far more important than differences in numbers of weapons or the total size of the opposing forces. It is difficult to take proper account of this effect—especially in a study such as this one, in which capabilities are considered in a highly aggregate fashion.

Finally, decisions regarding strategic forces are often the product of institutional biases and organizational interests that have developed over time in various government agencies and the military services. The type of analysis developed in this paper cannot account for these factors in projecting future courses of action. We are concerned with the optimum course, given a clear statement of goals and criteria, rather than with predicting the course the nation's strategic posture is most likely to follow.

Increased Expenditures for Strategic Forces

If the United States were to allocate more funds for strategic forces than the annual average of $20.2 billion mentioned above, it could meet several objectives not achieved in the present program.

• One option would be to implement programs to improve the military flexibility of the strategic force. These programs, which would be compatible with the SALT agreements, would focus on the development and deployment of a new generation of land- and sea-based missiles capable of greater accuracy, of higher yields, and of maneuvering on reentry. (The doctrinal and political implications of such developments were discussed in Chapter 2.) In brief, the new weapons—being designed to destroy hardened and defended military targets—would increase the military flexibility of U.S. strategic forces and thus give the United States greater warfighting capability, should deterrence fail. But since these weapons could also be used in a preemptive first strike against Soviet land-based strategic missiles, they could jeopardize the stability of a strategic relationship based on deterrence through secure retaliatory capabilities.

We cannot estimate the cost of such a program, for there is little information on the precise characteristics of the systems that would be developed or the number of missiles that would be procured, and much of the cost of reentry systems would be borne by the AEC. As a benchmark, one might note that the Minuteman III program costs roughly $10 million to $15 million per launcher, including missile procurement, silo modification, and research and development.

• A second higher-cost option would diversify the offensive force from a Triad to a force with four or five components. This move, reflecting a fundamental change in strategic doctrine, would be designed to increase confidence in U.S. retaliatory capabilities and to stabilize the strategic relationship by reducing the importance of any one system. Proponents of this alternative argue that developments in Soviet offensive missile technology, air defense, and antisubmarine warfare technology combine to threaten the present elements of the U.S. strategic offensive force. Diversification could be accomplished within the constraints of the SALT agreements, and some argue that it would give the Soviets incentives to agree to more comprehensive and restrictive limits on offensive weapons in the future. Defense Department spokesmen advanced this view in requesting $20 million for development of a submarine-launched cruise missile in June 1972. (The Congress authorized one-half the amount requested.)

Two new systems would be prime candidates for development: a large subsonic bomber carrying standoff missiles, and a submarine carrying relatively long-range (greater than 1,000 nautical miles) cruise missiles. Development of Trident would continue as currently scheduled, to maintain pressure on Soviet resources allocated to the development of counterweapons. B-1 development would continue, though at a slower pace, and a procurement decision would be postponed. Air defense modernization and ABM deployments would continue as previously planned.

The average annual cost of this program would be some $20.6 billion— about $400 million more than our projection of the present strategic program. The incremental costs would be higher at the end of the decade, however, and would continue to increase in the 1980s.

• A third higher-cost option would aim at increasing the U.S. advantage in warheads and bombers, to ease the political consequences imputed to the superior number of offensive missile launchers permitted the Soviet Union under the Interim Agreement. To be effective, this approach would require appropriate emphasis in the public pronouncements of U.S. officials.

The program would accelerate development of the B-1. The Trident program would remain as scheduled, since its present pace seems to be the fastest feasible. Air defense modernization, the Minuteman III program, and ABM deployments would all continue as currently planned.

Costs are estimated at about $20.8 billion a year—$600 million more than the projected annual cost of the present strategic posture. Again, the incremental costs would tend to grow with time.

Reduced Expenditures for Strategic Forces

To reduce the amount spent for strategic forces, the United States would have to give up some military or political capabilities, whether real or imagined. Strategic force costs could be reduced in three ways—by reducing air defenses, slowing weapon modernization, or reducing offensive force levels. The last could be done by eliminating one or two components of the Triad, or by cutting forces within the Triad structure.

• Curtailing strategic air defense would be an attractive way of saving money in the strategic budget. In advocating this course, one challenges neither official U.S. strategic doctrine nor present official judgments regarding the political efficacy of strategic forces. Quite simply, the argument rests on the limited nature of the strategic threat posed by the Soviet bomber force and on the futility of protecting American cities against that force while renouncing population defenses against Soviet missiles.

Reducing continental air defenses as described in Chapter 3 would provide savings averaging $900 million a year through fiscal 1980. This action would entail reductions in present surface-to-air missile and interceptor force levels and delays in modernization programs—the improved manned interceptor and AWACS.[2] These cuts would lower the average overall cost of the strategic force to $19.3 billion a year during fiscal 1974–80.

• Another way to cut strategic costs without reducing offensive capabilities, challenging present strategic doctrine, or questioning the political consequences of force level disparities, would be to slow down modernization. However, this option would discount the "bargaining chip" argument by downgrading the perceived value of development programs as incentives for the Soviet Union to reach arms control agreements. More importantly, it would suggest a downgrading of official U.S. public evaluations of Soviet technological progress. It would reflect confidence that present U.S. weapons are sufficiently superior to their Soviet counterparts and that they could perform the strategic retaliatory mission despite foreseeable improvements

---

2. Because these systems have military roles other than in strategic air defense, their development could continue. Their justification and costs, however, would have to be borne entirely by the general purpose force program.

in Soviet capabilities. Advocates of the option contend that fundamental deficiencies in technology—for example, in computers and in metallurgy—limit the Soviet Union's ability to develop more sophisticated weapons rapidly.

This option would complete the Minuteman and Poseidon MIRV deployments as now scheduled. Development of Trident and the B-1 would also continue, but their introduction into the operational force would be delayed three to five years, saving about $1.8 billion a year from fiscal 1974 through 1980. Much of these savings would be temporary, however, since total program costs would not decline nearly so sharply. Combining this slowdown in modernization with reductions in air defenses would reduce the average annual cost of the strategic force to $17.5 billion (in fiscal 1974–80), a saving of nearly $3 billion from projected costs of the existing program.

• To reduce the cost of the strategic posture without slowing the modernization of offensive forces, force levels could be reduced by eliminating weapon systems that contribute less to the U.S. deterrent, in proportion to their cost, than do other weapons. Adopting this option would imply that a heavy discount had been applied to arguments emphasizing the political consequences of force level imbalances in the belief that absolute capabilities, not relative numbers of launchers or platforms, were the important criteria for comparison.

The older B-52s (D models), the FB-111s, and their associated tankers would be phased out and the Minuteman II and Titan II missiles gradually retired. The Triad structure would be retained, since the newer bombers and the MIRVed Minuteman III missiles would remain in the force (no Minuteman II missiles would be MIRVed, of course). Lastly, this option would reduce air defense force levels and modernization rates as discussed previously.

The average annual cost of this program would also be about $17.5 billion—almost $3 billion less than our projection of the present program.

• An alternative way of reducing offensive force levels and costs would be to move away from the Triad structure. Adoption of this course would imply, as did the third option above, that a heavy discount had been applied to arguments regarding the political consequences of force level disparities. However, in accepting reductions in a single element of the Triad rather than across-the-board cuts, this option would place greater emphasis on the future vulnerability of the Minuteman force than on the benefits of redundancy. It would indicate that in agreeing to the SALT treaty limiting the deployment of ABM systems, the Defense Department had accepted the inevitable vulnerability of land-based missile systems. Viewing Minuteman vulnerability as potentially destabilizing, proponents of this course would phase out Minuteman and Titan as soon as Soviet offensive capabilities improved. The Minuteman III program would be halted immediately and the entire land-based force retired by 1980, thus changing the Triad to a Dyad. The Safeguard ABM system would be canceled immediately, though some ABM research and development would continue. Finally, the older B-52s and FB-111s would be retired.

To compensate for this decrease in U.S. offensive capabilities, the accelerated Trident development program would be maintained and plans made to increase the number of U.S. ballistic missile submarines when Trident becomes available in the 1980s. This approach would require that a SALT II agreement on offensive forces permit a shift from land- to sea-based missiles.

Gradually eliminating the Minuteman and Safeguard forces could save an average of $2.0 billion a year through fiscal 1980. Reductions in the bomber force would save another $1.2 billion. If these steps were combined with the reductions in air defense previously discussed, the overall annual cost of the strategic posture would decline to $16.1 billion—about $4 billion less than our projection of the present posture.

What We Buy with the Strategic Dollar

These illustrative strategic force options are summarized in Table 4-1. The table also includes a "minimum retaliatory force"—a strategic posture not discussed among the alternatives because we believe it would entail military and political risks too great for it to warrant serious consideration. This posture would move gradually to a completely sea-based force by completing the Poseidon program and maintaining Trident development on an accelerated schedule. All other modernization programs would be canceled; land-based missiles and strategic bombers would be phased out gradually, Safeguard terminated, and air defenses reduced to the surveillance role.

We include this single-element retaliatory force only to illustrate the minimum average cost of strategic forces for the rest of the seventies. That cost is unlikely to fall below $13 billion because of continuing requirements for research, surveillance, and command and control, in addition to costs of

Table 4-1. Average Annual Cost of Alternative Strategic Programs, Fiscal Years 1974–80

Total obligational authority in billions of constant 1974 dollars

Alternative	Land-based missiles	Sea-based missiles	Bombers	Air defenses, warning, and surveillance	Missile defenses	Civil defense	Total
Present posture	2.1	5.5	7.1	4.3	1.1	0.1	20.2
Higher-cost options							
Improve military flexibility	2.1+	5.5+	7.1	4.3	1.1	0.1	20.2+
Diversify offensive forces	2.1	5.7	7.3	4.3	1.1	0.1	20.6
Augment present offensive forces	2.1	5.5	7.7	4.3	1.1	0.1	20.8
Lower-cost options							
Reduce air defenses only	2.1	5.5	7.1	3.4	1.1	0.1	19.3
Slow down modernization	2.1	4.5	6.3	3.4	1.1	0.1	17.5
Eliminate less efficient forces	1.5	5.5	5.9	3.4	1.1	0.1	17.5
Move to a Dyad	0.6	5.5	5.9	3.4	0.6	0.1	16.1
Minimum retaliatory force	0.6	5.5	2.8	3.4	0.6	0.1	13.0

Source: Derived by authors.

the sea-based offensive force, and because any new departures must be made from an existing force structure. Even radical departures would have to be made gradually, both for efficiency and to minimize adverse domestic, military, and foreign policy effects.

This minimum sea-based force would cost one-third less than the average annual cost we project for the present posture from fiscal 1974 through 1980. Of course, costs at the end of the period would be considerably lower—probably on the order of $10 billion a year in 1980 as opposed to roughly $22 billion for the present posture, if both were expressed in fiscal 1974 dollars. Such a force could carry out the primary function of strategic forces as described in U.S. doctrine—to deter nuclear war by being able to absorb a preemptive attack and inflict unacceptable levels of damage to the attacker's population and industry in retaliation. But the other functions described in this paper would be jeopardized to an unacceptable degree.

Thus we are provided with a baseline to answer the question: What do we buy with our strategic dollar? Almost two-thirds of the annual $20.2 billion expenditure projected for 1974–80 will go to meet the minimum military requirements for a secure retaliatory capability. The remainder ($7.2 billion) serves three functions:

First, the United States buys added confidence in the ability of the strategic force to carry out the retaliatory mission, hence added confidence in the U.S. ability to deter nuclear war. About $4.5 billion of the difference between the minimum and projected postures can be accounted for by programs contributing to this function: completion of the Minuteman III program and maintenance of the MIRVed portion of the Minuteman force; completion and maintenance of the present Safeguard program; maintenance of the most capable part of the strategic bomber force—the B-52G–H models—and the B-1 replacement program. These forces and development programs serve primarily as hedges against the possible development of Soviet ASW forces capable of destroying a large part of the U.S. strategic submarine force in a preemptive strike. They also complicate the problems the Soviets would face if they sought to obtain a preemptive capability and cause them to diffuse their research funds among several forces and technologies. These programs thus can be viewed primarily as forms of insurance. Evaluation of them must be subjective, based on one's propensity for risk-taking.

Second, the United States avoids the adverse political consequences sometimes attributed to major unilateral force reductions. These consequences, said to result from an adverse change in the generalized image of the relative strength of the United States and the Soviet Union held by each other and by third nations, include a reduction in incentives for the Soviet Union to negotiate seriously on arms control and other topics of mutual interest, an increase in Soviet propensities toward hostile behavior, and reduced confidence among U.S. allies in the value of U.S. defense commitments—leading, at worst, toward neutralism or toward pressures for national nuclear weapon programs in Western Europe and Japan. Many of the programs listed in the preceding paragraph can be said to avert these adverse political effects while contributing to confidence in American retaliatory capabilities. Some programs, however, would seem to be justified on a political basis alone. The latter include maintenance of the least efficient parts of the offensive strategic force—Minuteman II and Titan missiles, the older model B-52s, and the FB-111 bombers. These forces account for $1.8 billion of the difference between costs of the minimum force and projected costs of the present posture.

The remaining $0.9 billion of the difference between the two postures is used to maintain and modernize a strategic air defense force whose capabilities exceed those required by the surveillance role. This expenditure seems attributable more to the momentum of ongoing programs and organizational interests, and to a diffuse fear of leaving the nation without active defenses against air attack, than to the dictates of strategic doctrine.

In Conclusion

Any judgment of the "right" amount to spend on strategic forces depends ultimately on subjective evaluations of the dollar values to be attached to redundancy in U.S. retaliatory forces, to flexibility in U.S. nuclear warfighting capabilities, to avoidance of the political costs of force level disparities, and to the other considerations discussed above. Many variables and uncertainties are necessarily involved in this type of judgment. With this caution, we report our own views.

We believe that the cost of strategic forces could be reduced without jeopardizing their retaliatory capability and without adverse political consequences for the United States. The SALT agreements, with their implied acceptance of mutual deterrence and overall parity, seem to us to provide a basis for economies in strategic spending. Although the rivalry in strategic weapons certainly will continue, the possibilities for restraint and for better understanding seem to have increased.

The preferred strategic posture, as we see it, would emphasize the requirements for strategic stability, maintain adequate hedges against developments that would threaten the U.S. retaliatory capability, and emphasize qualitative as well as quantitative comparisons between American and Soviet forces, thus reducing the emphasis currently placed on the political consequences of force level disparities. What would this posture imply?

Strategic Stability

The goal of strategic stability has two major implications.

First, it would seem to rule out some of the improvements in strategic missiles requested by the Defense Department in spring 1972. These characteristics—greater accuracy and payload and the capability to maneuver on reentry—though useful to improve military flexibility for warfighting should deterrence fail, would also give the impression of attempting to attain a preemptive first-strike capability. We believe that increasing the military flexibility of the strategic force at the expense of increasing Soviet apprehension as to American intentions would be a poor tradeoff.

Second, strategic stability would seem to require that land-based missiles be eliminated from the strategic force over the long term. This move should be completed before the Soviet Union could deploy a first-strike capability against the Minuteman force, probably early in the next decade. In the interim, we would recommend completion of the Minuteman III program at a level of 550 launchers and of the Safeguard system at one site. No follow-on land-based missile system should be developed, and the U.S. negotiators in SALT II should emphasize transferring land-based missiles to sea.

Maintaining Confidence

To maintain confidence in the U.S. retaliatory capability, our preferred strategic posture would continue to develop follow-on systems to succeed the present force of manned bombers and strategic submarines, as does the present program. However, we recommend modifications in each development program.

We would slow the B-1 development program somewhat and begin parallel development of a standoff bomber. The decision as to which new bomber to procure would be delayed until the relative capabilities and costs of penetrating as against standoff systems could be more fully evaluated.

Unless evidence concerning Soviet ASW programs suggests a need to introduce the Trident submarine before the early 1980s, we would slow the pace of Trident development in the interest of evolving the design best suited to counter likely developments in Soviet ASW capability and to minimize the real cost per unit. The pace of Trident development envisioned in fiscal 1972 seems appropriate to us.

Political Consequences

In our view, the political consequences of changes in military force levels reflect a diffuse and highly generalized impression of the effect of changes in real military power. Within very wide bounds of relative military potential, this impression is as much the result of qualitative changes in weapon characteristics and, more importantly, of the statements and behavior of national leaders—the will they demonstrate, the reasons they give for the changes, the emphasis they put on various measures of military strength, and so forth—as it is of simplistic comparisons of relative numbers of weapons. We consider this to be particularly true with regard to nuclear weapons, since the cost of using those weapons is clearly and generally perceived as catastrophic to both the "winner" and the "loser" of any conflict. Only if the quantitative disparity is large and dramatic are adverse foreign policy effects likely to be felt; as the President suggested in his 1972 Foreign Policy Report to the Congress, modest disparities can be accepted without adverse effects.

Retiring the older model B-52 bombers, the FB-111 bomber force, their associated tankers, and the Minuteman II and Titan II missiles would represent a substantial reduction in force levels and provide considerable cost savings, with only marginal changes in the military capabilities of the strategic force. It would also be desirable, in our view, to reduce air defense force levels and moderate many air defense modernization programs, even if the political consequences were greater than expected.

All together, the decisions outlined above would result in a strategic posture that would cost, on the average, roughly $15.9 billion a year from fiscal 1974 through fiscal 1980. Although savings would peak near the middle of the decade and costs would tend to rise toward the end of the period, overall spending for strategic forces would decline about 20 percent from the level we project for the present program. It would do so, moreover, without jeopardizing any of the essential objectives that should, in our view, govern the nation's choices.

Some Determinants of Ballistic Missile Effectiveness

Comparisons of American and Soviet strategic forces are complicated by the differing characteristics and deployments of their missiles. Below are discussed some of the operational aspects and qualitative characteristics of ballistic missiles.

Range and Payload

The size of a ballistic missile's payload and the range at which it can be delivered depend primarily on the total impulse delivered by the missile booster. For a given size of booster, range and payload can be traded off. Thus it is possible to increase the maximum range of a missile by reducing the number or weight of the reentry vehicles. A practical limit to such potential range increases is imposed by the reentry vehicles, which are exposed to greater temperature effects on reentry from longer trajectories.

For fixed land-based ICBMs, range requirements depend on the distance from launch site to potential target areas. The following are the great circle map distances from a Minuteman launch point in northern North Dakota to possible targets (the earth's rotation during the flight of the missile affects the actual length of the trajectory):

	Range in nautical miles
Moscow	5,100
Sary Shagan (USSR missile test site)	6,000
Peking	5,700
Canton	6,100

For sea-based missiles, increases in range not only can provide greater target coverage but also can allow the submarine to increase its ocean deployment area while still covering the same set of targets. This can be illustrated by showing the ocean area[1] available to a ballistic missile submarine as a function of missile range from the Soviet capital, Moscow:

Submarine-launched missile range (nautical miles)	*Possible deployment area (millions of square nautical miles)*
1,000	1.0
2,000	3.0
3,000	6.5
4,000	14.5
5,000	27.5
6,000	42.5

Accuracy

Circular error probable (CEP) is the commonest measure of the accuracy with which a ballistic missile can deliver its reentry vehicles. It is defined as the radius of a circle centered on the target within which 50 percent of the reentry vehicles would impact if the test were repeated many times. Thus, if a ballistic missile system is said to have a CEP of 1 nautical mile, its reentry vehicles would have a 50 percent probability of landing within a circle of 1 nautical mile radius, centered on the target.

The guidance and control system is usually the main determinant of missile accuracy. In most modern missiles an inertial guidance system is used, sometimes assisted by radio or stellar navigation systems. Guidance systems consist of an inertial platform that provides stable directions of reference, accelerometers that continuously measure changes in velocity, and a computer that calculates the corrections necessary to direct the reentry vehicle to the target. These corrections are transmitted to the control system, which changes the flight path of the missile.

Still other factors affect the accuracy of the missile and the amount of error in the impact. The size of the error depends on the degree to which the following uncertainties can be resolved:
- The exact relative locations of the launch point and target.
- The effects of winds and deviations in atmospheric pressure during reentry.
- Variations in the earth's gravity field along the flight trajectory.
- Variations in the physical characteristics of the reentry vehicle (for example, weight and drag).

1. Excluding waters beneath the polar ice caps and within the 200 fathom line.

To attain high accuracies (that is, a CEP less than 0.25 nautical mile) without the use of terminal guidance, substantial scientific and engineering efforts are necessary to reduce the effects of these sources of error, and those efforts are confirmed with a large-scale test program.

Reliability and Yield

Reliability refers to the likelihood that a missile will successfully complete its mission, independently of enemy action. It is usually thought of in sequential terms: maintenance of the missile on alert, successful flight through boost and reentry, and successful warhead detonation. Because of the ban on atmospheric testing of nuclear weapons and other operational limitations, it is impossible to measure reliability through complete tests. Instead, information is collected from flight tests of missiles with inert warheads, from tests of components, and from underground nuclear tests, and combined to form estimates of overall system reliability. These estimates are not available to the public; however, one can speculate that a system with a reliability of less than 50 percent would clearly be unsatisfactory, while the engineering complexity of typical systems would place an upper limit of 90 to 95 percent on system reliability.

Yield is a measure of the destructiveness of the nuclear warhead, expressed as the number of tons of TNT that would liberate the same blast energy. The earliest nuclear weapons released about the same energy as 20 kilotons (thousands of tons) of TNT; a 1 megaton nuclear weapon would release the energy equivalent of 1 million tons of TNT. Yield expressed in equivalent megatons (EMT) has come into use as a measure of the urban or industrial area that could be destroyed by several nuclear weapons. It is expressed by the relationship $EMT = NY^{\frac{2}{3}}$, in which N is the number of weapons of yield Y. The lethal radius due to blast is proportional to the $\frac{1}{3}$ power of the yield and the area is proportional to the square of the lethal radius. If the yield is greater than 1 megaton, the $\frac{1}{2}$ power is used since weapons of that size would destroy an area larger than most urban centers.

Reentry Systems

The acronyms MRV, MIRV, and more recently MARV have been applied to reentry systems, but the differences in their characteristics have not always been made clear. Since the first generations of both U.S. and Soviet missiles carried only a single reentry vehicle, the confusion concerns newer missiles.

The term multiple reentry vehicle (MRV) refers to a system that has more than one warhead; however, the warheads are delivered in a cluster like pellets from a shotgun. They are released from the booster at nearly the same instant and at the same velocity, and follow almost identical trajectories. For practical purposes, they must all be directed at the same target. The Polaris A-3 missile is an example of an MRV system; according to newspaper reports, the SS-9 triplet system that was tested extensively by the Soviet Union in 1969–70 is of the same type.[2]

Multiple independently targetable reentry vehicles (MIRVs) involve much more sophisticated technology in that each vehicle must be accurately placed on a different trajectory. This enables the warheads to be directed to separate targets within the booster's "footprint"—that is, the geographic area within which possible targets of a given combination of missile and reentry system must be contained. One technique designed to achieve this MIRV capability uses the so-called bus system. Here, a master guidance system and the last stage of the propulsion system maneuver to release each reentry vehicle on a separate trajectory. (A possible variation would be to place a separate guidance and propulsion system on each reentry vehicle, but this technique would be costly and has not yet appeared in an operational system.) Poseidon and Minuteman III are operational MIRV systems using buses; the Trident missile now under development also will carry MIRVs.

A new type of reentry system called MARV, for *ma*neuvering *r*eentry vehicle, has been discussed in connection with the Trident program.[3] Such a vehicle would be designed to maneuver during reentry into the atmosphere, probably by the use of aerodynamic flaps. The object would be to improve penetration of ABM defenses by making it extremely difficult to predict and intercept the reentry flight path.

2. Michael Getler, "Russian Missile Faulted," *Washington Post*, June 17, 1971.

3. *Fiscal Year 1973 Authorization for Military Procurement, Research and Development, Construction Authorization for the Safeguard ABM, and Active Duty and Selected Reserve Strengths*, Hearings before the Senate Armed Services Committee, 92 Cong. 2 sess. (1972), Pt. 5, pp. 3196 and 3205.

APPENDIX B

The Problem of Minuteman Vulnerability

It is generally agreed in the analytical community that the Minuteman force would become vulnerable to a first strike *if* the Soviets chose to allocate a large part of their ICBM capability to that task *and* made improvements in missile accuracy and MIRV technology.

The following graph, supplied by the chairman of the Joint Chiefs of Staff, Admiral Thomas H. Moorer, to the Senate Armed Services Committee in 1972, illustrates the capability the Soviets would have to achieve to attack the Minuteman force successfully. The graph shows the probability that a penetrating warhead (of various yields) would destroy a Minuteman silo as a function of missile accuracy (CEP). If the Soviets MIRVed each of their 300 SS-9s with three warheads, each of 5 megaton (MT) yield, they could count on delivering about 675 warheads, assuming a nominal 0.75 reliability for the system. If the SS-9 were accurate within 0.5 mile, each penetrating warhead have about a 0.7 probability of success, and about 475 Minuteman silos would be destroyed. However, more than 500 Minuteman missiles would survive, leaving the United States with a substantial deterrent capability in ICBMs alone. If the Soviets reduced their CEP to 0.2 mile, 325 Minuteman missiles would survive.

If one assumes that the Soviets could mount a force containing some 5,000 warheads of 1 MT each, the situation becomes more threatening. It is possible, given the payload capability of their large missiles, that they could place about 15 warheads in the 1 MT range on each SS-9, yielding about 4,500 warheads. The 970 SS-11 missiles are estimated to carry a single 1 MT warhead each, bringing the total to more than 5,000.[1] In such a case the Soviets could target about 5 warheads against each Minuteman silo.

1. International Institute for Strategic Studies, *The Military Balance, 1971–1972* (London: IISS, 1971), p. 57.

75

Figure B-1. Threat to Minuteman

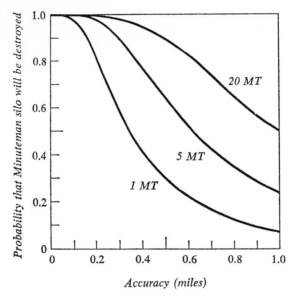

Source: Fiscal Year 1973 Authorization for Military Procurement, Research and Development, Construction Authorization for the Safeguard ABM, and Active Duty and Selected Reserve Strengths, Hearings before the Senate Armed Services Committee, 92 Cong. 2 sess. (1972), Pt. 2, p. 554.

Again assuming a reliability[2] of 0.75 and a CEP of 0.5 mile, only 250 Minuteman silos would survive. If the Soviets reduced their CEP to 0.2 mile, only 10 Minuteman silos would remain.

The Air Force is optimistic that Minuteman will be effective through the seventies. In 1972, Secretary of the Air Force Robert Seamans testified before the Senate Armed Services Committee:

We, of course, recognize that we want to improve Minuteman survivability, but we feel that the Minuteman today is a very significant deterrent. You have a thousand of these missiles, there are over [deleted] of them at any one time that are ready to go. . . .

I think that the program that we have here for increasing survivability, both of the missile itself once it leaves the hole as well as of the launch site, will provide a deterrent at the end of the seventies.[3]

2. In these calculations the Soviets are not credited with a capability to retarget to compensate for unreliable missiles.

3. *Fiscal Year 1973 Authorization for Military Procurement, Research and Development, Construction Authorization for the Safeguard ABM, and Active Duty and Selected Reserve Strengths,* Hearings before the Senate Armed Services Committee, 92 Cong. 2 sess. (1972), Pt. 2, pp. 1165–66.

However, before the same committee Dr. John S. Foster, director of Defense Research and Engineering, was less sanguine:

I believe that the Minuteman weapon system will be viable into the 1980's if we can provide an adequate level of survivability. Senator Stennis, I honestly believe that there is a risk that too few Minutemen might be surviving in [deleted] even if we go ahead with Safeguard and even if we go ahead with site defense of Minuteman as planned. Let me say why. The Soviets have made a fair investment already in their SS-9s and SS-11s. Modifications of one or both of those, made very quickly and rapidly deployed, could reduce the available number of retaliatory Minuteman below a critical level by [deleted] even with our best efforts. On the other hand, while we have slipped in our Safeguard deployment, the Soviets in their ABM program have also slipped. I would hope that, with our planned efforts, we would be able to maintain a viable deterrent in the Minuteman system; but one cannot guarantee it.[4]

The SALT Interim Agreement does not prohibit the Soviet Union from developing an accurate MIRV. Given the Soviet potential to develop the necessary technology, it appears that no steps permissible under the agreement (such as silo hardening) could greatly improve confidence in Minuteman's survivability in the long term. The agreement allows so few Safeguard interceptor missiles that they would be quickly overwhelmed by a massive Soviet MIRV attack. It should be acknowledged that the same would be true even for a full-scale Safeguard program. The Site Defense of Minuteman (SDM) program is limited by SALT to research and development because of problems associated with verification and with the proliferation of radars for a deployed system. In any event, SDM defensive missiles could not be deployed in significant quantities until the early 1980s even if they were permitted by a SALT II agreement.

A more optimistic view of the Minuteman vulnerability problem suggests that SALT II may provide some relief. The Soviets may be concerned about the survivability of their own land-based ICBMs, given the American lead in MIRVs and warhead technology and the improved accuracies of the latest generation of U.S. missiles. Thus there may be a mutual interest in a solution to the problem.

Some possible approaches to reducing the vulnerability of ICBMs in future agreements would be to:

• Limit the number of missiles that could be MIRVed to a level that is not threatening. It should be recalled, however, that such limitations could not be verified by existing unilateral means.

4. *Ibid.*, Pt. 3, p. 1862.

- Limit the number of missile flight tests. Both the United States and the Soviet Union conduct extensive flight tests of new missile systems to identify technical and operational problems and to gain confidence in the performance of the entire system. Unilateral verification of the number of flight tests would present fewer obstacles than would a limit on the number of MIRVs. Some believe that by curtailing flight tests, neither side would have sufficient confidence in its missiles to rely on them for a first strike. Whether confidence in their *retaliatory* capability would be reduced to unacceptable levels is an important judgment that would have to be made.

Putting aside the destabilizing aspects of Minuteman vulnerability, a case can be made that land-based missiles have a utility that is worth their future costs. They are potentially useful in a limited war in which a premium would be placed on rapid and responsive command and control and on flexibility in target selection. Existence of the Minuteman force also poses problems for the Soviets in planning a simultaneous attack on both U.S. missile sites and bomber bases. If the Soviets should plan a first strike with a simultaneous impact of ICBMs and SLBMs on American strategic bases, they would have to plan to launch their ICBMs at least 15 minutes earlier than their SLBMs. Since new U.S. surveillance systems would detect and report the launch of Soviet ICBMs immediately, the United States would have time to place its alert bombers in the air and to prepare its own missile force for launch.[5]

5. This capability is attributed to the Program 647 satellite and the Program 313 relay satellite. Alex Galloway, "A Decade of U.S. Reconnaissance Satellites," *International Defense Review* (Geneva), Vol. 5 (English edition, June 1972), p. 253.

Some Considerations in Strategic Antisubmarine Warfare

Both the United States and the Soviet Union devote sizable research facilities, naval forces, and financial and manpower resources to the problems of antisubmarine warfare (ASW). Each has developed a variety of weapons and sensors to perform the tasks of ASW, and these systems are deployed on many kinds of platforms—attack submarines, land-based patrol aircraft, escort ships, mines, and ship-based helicopters. But at present, only the United States maintains ship-based fixed-wing aircraft and fixed underwater detection systems in both the Atlantic and the Pacific.

Although it is difficult to assign precise cost estimates to ASW, principally because most naval platforms serve multiple purposes, it is clear that each superpower is making a large investment. A marketing study made in late 1972 indicated that American spending on ASW would rise from $2.5 billion in that year to $4.5 billion by fiscal 1975.[1] Another study, taking a broader view of the share of naval resources that should be charged to ASW, estimated that the United States has spent at least $8 billion a year for forces whose primary mission is antisubmarine warfare.[2]

While both the American Polaris/Poseidon fleet and the Soviet Union's force of Yankee-class submarines appear to be relatively invulnerable to ASW at present, the large investment each nation is making in ASW could eventually threaten the submarine-launched ballistic missile deterrent. For this threat to be realized, however, a great many technical and tactical problems would have to be solved.

In considering them, one must make a sharp distinction between the problems of strategic ASW and those of ASW in protection of naval forces

1. *New York Times*, October 20, 1972.
2. Charles L. Schultze and others, *Setting National Priorities: The 1972 Budget* (Brookings Institution, 1971), p. 55.

or merchant shipping. The latter mission, generally known as "sea control," has been the primary focus of ASW research since the First World War. But strategic ASW is the more challenging problem, for two reasons:

First, in the sea control problem the submarine plays an active role as the attacker. It must position itself within torpedo or cruise missile range of the commercial or naval target, thus delimiting the area that must be searched by ASW forces. In maneuvering to attack its target, the submarine makes a certain amount of noise and otherwise indicates its presence. On the other hand, the strategic submarine can usually remain passive until shortly before it launches its missiles; moreover, it can do so under large areas of ocean.

Second, the damage potential of submarines engaged in conventional warfare is much less and the value of their individual targets lower than would be the case in strategic nuclear war. Because the stakes of individual engagements are smaller, a conventional ASW effort can be effective if it only depletes the enemy submarine force over a period of many months. For strategic ASW to be effective, particularly as part of a preemptive attack, it must destroy a large part of the opposing deployed strategic submarines nearly simultaneously and before they can launch their missiles. The price of missing even one submarine could be extraordinarily high. Finally, the strategic ASW mission must be performed without alerting the target nation's command system, since warning the adversary would increase the difficulty of staging a successful disarming strike against the other components of his strategic force.

Detecting and precisely locating submerged submarines is a formidable task because seawater does not transmit light or electromagnetic signals over long distances. Conversely, acoustic signals are transmitted much faster and farther in seawater than in air. However, sound waves passing through seawater are distorted by effects of the ocean floor and by temperature and pressure gradients in the water. The sound of the target may be concealed by background noises from such sources as waves, marine life, and surface ships.

Despite these handicaps, the U.S. Navy has relied primarily on acoustic means (sonar) to detect and locate submerged submarines, and the Soviet Union appears to be doing the same. Acoustic detection can be effective in conventional sea control missions for the reasons cited above, but it is likely to be less effective in strategic antisubmarine warfare. By reducing its speed, a strategic submarine can lower its radiated noise to a level below the background noise of the ocean. Because of the greater ranges involved, it is hard to get accurate bearing and range information even if a target is detected. Nonacoustic means of detection have been investigated—lasers, magnetic detectors, and infrared detectors being among those that have come to public attention.[3] At present, however, their range appears very limited, and they offer little promise of penetrating the opaque ocean.

Even if the problems of detecting and locating strategic submarines were solved, the question of launching an effective coordinated attack on them would remain. Torpedoes or depth charges dropped from aircraft are possible weapons; a barrage by nuclear-armed missiles could be used if information on the location of the submarines could be transmitted from the sensor to the missile launchers accurately and with a low rate of false contacts.

As the foregoing discussion suggests, the larger the area that must be searched for a submarine, the more difficult the ASW task becomes. Therein lies the main rationale for increasing the range of submarine-launched ballistic missiles (SLBMs) and with it the ocean areas available for strategic submarine deployment. The urgency of this objective depends on one's view of the seriousness and imminence of a Soviet ASW threat.

The advantage to be gained by increasing SLBM range is modified somewhat once the possibility of "trailing" is considered. This tactic, an alternative to the large area search and localization approach, would employ attack submarines to trail strategic submarine targets at a distance that would permit the attacker to close and sink the target quickly. The trailing submarine would solve the detection and localization problem by picking up the quarry at its home base as it was starting a patrol or at a chokepoint such as the Greenland–Iceland–United Kingdom gap. Trailing would be attempted with passive sonars in the hope of not alerting the strategic submarine target; use of active sonars would immediately warn the quarry of the attacker's presence.

Measures are available to counter a trailing threat. The strategic submarine can be accompanied by escort ships to monitor its departure from home ports, and it can use acoustic decoys combined with evasive tactics in order to break a trail. By slowing to very low speeds, it can reduce its

3. For a detailed discussion of nonacoustic techniques, see International Institute for Strategic Studies, *The Strategic Survey, 1970* (London: IISS, 1970), pp. 14–15. For an unclassified state-of-the-art discussion of ASW, see Richard L. Garwin, "Anti-submarine Warfare and National Security," *Scientific American*, Vol. 227 (July 1972).

radiated noise level below background noise, making passive trailing impossible and aiding in detection of the trailing submarine.

American antisubmarine warfare technology is considered more advanced than that currently possessed by the Soviet Union, and U.S. submarines are generally considered to be qualitatively superior to their Soviet counterparts.[4] Consequently it is widely accepted that the Soviet Union does not now have a capability to endanger the Polaris/Poseidon fleet. As this discussion has indicated, the Soviets would face severe technological and tactical obstacles in attempting to achieve such a capability in the future.

4. For example, in their respective radiated noise levels. William Beecher, "New Soviet Subs Relatively Noisy, Easy to Detect," *New York Times*, October 9, 1969.

Effectiveness of the Bomber Force

Stated in terms of military effectiveness, the objective of the bomber force is to hold hostage a large number of enemy targets, primarily cities, through the capability to deliver nuclear warheads on them. The term *hostage* is used because, as a part of the concept of deterrence, it is hoped that the capability to deliver the weapons will never be exercised.

Bombers are best suited to targets such as cities that do not change in value over time. Targets such as enemy missile silos and airfields are time-urgent in the sense that their vehicles (missiles or bombers) presumably would be launched minutes after initiation of a nuclear war. Bombers have a long flight time (several hours from launch to weapon delivery) as opposed to minutes for missiles (about 15 minutes for SLBMs and 30 minutes for ICBMs). Thus, in most circumstances, bombers would arrive too late to be effective against missile silos and airfields.

Four conditions and events affect the capability of the bomber force to deliver nuclear weapons on targets: (1) prelaunch survivability, (2) penetration of enemy area air defenses, (3) penetration of enemy terminal defenses, and (4) destruction potential. In the following sections, these factors are considered primarily in the context of the potential Soviet threat, with secondary attention to China.

Prelaunch Survivability

A preemptive attack by the Soviet Union on American bomber bases with ballistic missiles constitutes the only serious threat to the survivability of U.S. bomber forces until they reach enemy territory. The Soviet Union undoubtedly could destroy nearly all of the more than 40 bomber and tanker bases in the United States[1] through a coordinated attack using only a small number (about 100) of its ICBMs. Because most airfield installations and the aircraft parked on them are highly vulnerable to the blast from nuclear weapons, a single delivered weapon of the yield and accuracy attributed to the Soviet missile arsenal would destroy everything on the ground.

The United States seeks to counter this ballistic missile threat by maintaining

• detection systems that warn of the launch or flight of enemy missiles,

• a sizable number of aircraft in a state of sufficient readiness on the ground that they can be quickly launched after warning and fly out a safe distance from their air base, and

• a command and control network that transmits the warning, orders the bombers to launch, and directs them to their targets.

For many years the detection system consisted solely of the ballistic missile early warning system (BMEWS), which had large radars located in Alaska, Greenland, and England. More recently, over-the-horizon radars have given the United States the capability to detect missiles early in their trajectory, and a new satellite surveillance system contributes an ability to detect the launch of enemy missiles.[2] Thus the Strategic Air Command would receive about 30 minutes' warning before the impact of warheads from Soviet ICBMs. It is important to note that warning systems need not be infallible with respect to false alarms on the flight of enemy ICBMs. A virtue of U.S. bomber survivability measures is that the aircraft can be launched and recalled in case of a false alarm.

At present about 40 percent of the bomber and tanker force is in a state of readiness or alert that would enable those aircraft to be launched before their home bases were destroyed.[3] Aircraft not on alert would not be expected to survive. The ratio of alert aircraft to the inventory force can be increased, but a feasible upper limit for a continuous alert is about 60 percent because some aircraft must be rotated through periodic inspections and used for combat readiness training of the air crews. Higher rates can be

1. *Department of Defense Appropriations for 1972*, Hearings before a Subcommittee of the House Committee on Appropriations, 92 Cong. 1 sess. (1971), Pt. 6, p. 304.

2. *Ibid.*

3. *Military Implications of the Treaty on the Limitation of Anti-Ballistic Missile Systems and the Interim Agreement on Limitation of Strategic Offensive Arms*, Hearing before the Senate Armed Services Committee, 92 Cong. 2 sess. (1972), p. 474.

achieved and held in a crisis of a few weeks' duration. At times of extreme tension, such as the Cuban missile crisis, U.S. leaders have resorted to putting some of the bombers into the air on alert. An airborne alert ensures survivability and demonstrates U.S. concern over the seriousness of the situation, but it is expensive to maintain more than a few days.

Since 1971 a new kind of threat has been conceived that could place far greater strain on the present warning and launch system.[4] It would consist in the deployment close to American shores—say within 100 miles—of Soviet Yankee-class submarines armed with missiles designed to follow an unusually low (depressed) trajectory. By depressing the trajectory, the missiles' flight time from launch to impact would be cut from 15 minutes to only 7 minutes over the 1,000-mile range needed to reach many U.S. bomber bases. The missiles would be launched at distant targets first and at the high rate of about four per minute, so that even with reliable detection and transmission of the information, U.S. bombers would have at most 6 minutes to react before being destroyed.

The Air Force states that there is "absolutely no evidence that the Soviets are developing depressed trajectory SLBMs, or that they would risk stationing their ballistic missile submarines close to our shores. . . ."[5] No evidence available to the public indicates that the Soviets will try to achieve such a capability for their SLBMs; however, their current high production rate of Yankee-class ballistic missile submarines could culminate in a force of up to 62 modern submarines under the Interim Agreement. With a force of that size, the Soviets might be able to keep about 20 missile submarines stationed continuously off the coasts of the United States. Existing U.S. intelligence sensors could be counted on to warn if the Soviets deployed submarines in this manner or performed the necessary extensive testing of depressed trajectory missiles.

This conception of the SLBM threat poses severe but not insurmountable problems for survivability of the bomber force. If necessary, the reaction time of the bombers could be reduced by placing aircraft near the ends of runways, keeping crews in or near the aircraft, and modifying the jet engines to allow faster starts. Further dispersal inland would make it more difficult for the Soviets to attack the airfields simultaneously. Lastly, some of the bombers and their supporting tankers could be kept in the air con-

4. Captain James A. Winnefeld and Carl H. Builder, "ASW—Now or Never," United States Naval Institute, *Proceedings*, Vol. 97 (September 1971), p. 21.

5. *Department of Defense Appropriations for 1972*, House Hearings, Pt. 6, pp. 303–04.

tinuously. This measure would be expensive, but it would guarantee survivability of the alert force.

Countermeasures involving other forces also have been proposed. One of them—a modified Safeguard system to defend bomber bases—is now precluded by the Moscow accords. Another proposal[6] calls for the use of conventional antisubmarine forces to deny the Soviets the capability described above. Such measures would be riskier, more likely to provoke a Soviet reaction, and more expensive than steps that involved changes only in the bomber force.

Penetration of Soviet Area Air Defenses

Once U.S. bomber and tanker aircraft have been launched, little can affect their mission until they near the enemy mainland. Orders committing them to attack a given set of targets would be issued by radio en route. A complicating factor is the need to refuel bombers in the air, as close as possible to enemy territory but before enemy air defenses could be brought to bear. Failure in refueling would cause some of the bombers to abort or change their mission, a possibility reflected in estimates of bomber reliability.

Penetrating bombers probably would interact first with the enemy area air defenses. The key element in those defenses is the fighter/interceptor, equipped with sensors and missiles and supported by a ground radar network and command and control system. The "ground environment" detects and identifies the attacking bombers, establishes their track, and directs fighters into a position to locate and attack the bombers. This capability could also be carried aloft in a so-called airborne warning and control system (AWACS), a large, transport-like aircraft equipped with large radars.

How well these defensive systems perform depends largely on the extent to which they can detect, identify, track, and attack low-flying penetrators. The problems of achieving this "look down, shoot down" capability are exceptionally difficult, especially over land. Radars must be designed to reject objects that do not move, while detecting relatively small moving targets in the cluttered image reflected from the land.

Bombers can use several tactics and devices that assist in penetrating area defenses. Flying as close to the ground as the guidance system will per-

6. Winnefeld and Builder, "ASW—Now or Never," p. 25.

mit greatly reduces the coverage of enemy ground radars, since they operate by line of sight. Airborne radars are confronted with the problem of distinguishing a bomber target from ground clutter. U.S. bombers are also equipped with electronic countermeasures designed to jam or deceive enemy radars. In addition the bomber can launch decoys like the unarmed Quail or, in the future, the subsonic cruise armed decoy (SCAD), which are designed to appear the same as the mother bomber to enemy radars. This tactic would dilute the defenses by presenting many different targets, saturating the command and control system with intersecting tracks.

These various offensive and defensive measures interact to make estimating the effectiveness of bombers in this phase a formidable task. External factors such as weather, time of day, geography, and the possibility of an early missile attack add uncertainties that could negate the best of estimates. However, two generalizations seem applicable to the relationship between some of the important variables of the bomber penetration equation:

• Diluting enemy defenses by increasing the number of credible penetrators (either bombers or decoys) improves penetration capability by a factor of more than one, assuming, of course, that all other factors are constant.
• The farther a bomber must penetrate into enemy territory, the less likely will be the success of the mission, since the bomber will be progressively exposed to more defenses.

During the past two decades the Soviet Union has made large investments in its air defense system, building an extensive network of ground radars and a force of about 3,000 interceptor aircraft. The most impressive of the interceptors is the Mig-23 (Foxbat), which holds two world speed records.[7] However, nothing in the public record indicates that the Soviets have achieved or even attempted to achieve a "look down, shoot down" capability in their interceptors. Until they do develop that technology, low-flying U.S. bombers and air-to-surface missiles will remain relatively invulnerable to Soviet area air defenses.

Thus the urgency attached to the SCAD program depends on judgments as to the time when the Soviets might gain a "look down, shoot down" capability. At present, SCAD would offer the best chance of countering that threat. Electronic countermeasures carried by the bomber cost less but provide less confidence. The B-1 is being designed to fly faster and hundreds of feet lower than the B-52, and to present a much smaller radar

7. *Department of Defense Appropriations for 1972*, House Hearings, Pt. 2, p. 246.

target (nose on) than the B-52. But these improvements would only marginally increase penetration of the bomber itself against a combination of
an advanced interceptor and AWACS. The key to penetration is the dilu-
tion and confusion of defenses with SCAD; both the B-1 and B-52 will depend on SCAD for survival if a high quality Soviet air defense system
should emerge during their service lives.

Penetration of Terminal Air Defenses and SAM Barriers

Terminal air defenses consist of surface-to-air missiles (SAMs), radars
that detect, track, and identify the target, and a command and control system. The missile accelerates quickly to high velocities to intercept the target.
In most systems it is guided to the target by ground radar; it can, however,
be equipped with a sensor (a small self-contained radar or heat seeker) to
guide it during the final part of its intercept. The warhead may be either a
conventional high explosive or nuclear, though the detonation of nuclear
warheads at low altitude would cause considerable damage to the defended
area.

Antiaircraft guns usually are not considered an effective terminal defense in strategic nuclear war because of their limited range and payload.
On the other hand, high-energy lasers might eventually be used in a low-
altitude terminal defense system, their advantage being the essentially zero
flight time of the laser beam. The feasibility of such a system would depend
on its costs, power requirements, kill mechanisms, and the effects of the
atmosphere on the laser beam.

Several factors determine the performance of any terminal defense system: radar coverage as related to the altitude of the target; the minimum
altitude below which no engagement can take place; the reaction time from
detection to launch of the interceptor and the refire time between launches;
the number of targets that can be handled simultaneously; and velocity of
the interceptor.

Certain characteristics and capabilities of the penetrator (bomber or air-
to-surface missile) also affect the outcome of an engagement with terminal
defenses: the size of the radar cross-section (image) the penetrator presents;
its speed, altitude, and maneuvering; and the quality of its electronic countermeasures.

The penetrator can evade detection by flying outside the radar coverage or defeat the defenses by flying below their minimum altitude capability. Consequently, intelligence information on the location of defensive batteries and their minimum altitude capability becomes paramount in planning how to penetrate defenses. If the penetrator combines high speed with a small radar cross-section, it is difficult for the defense to react in time following initial detection.

The Air Force at present relies on flying at low altitude and maneuvering to avoid surface-to-air missile sites that are not in the immediate vicinity of the target.[8] Its short-range attack missile (SRAM) is specifically designed for situations in which terminal defenses must be penetrated or suppressed in order to reach the target. The SRAM combines a small radar cross-section with high velocity, but at limited range; thus it is expected to fly to and destroy a SAM battery before even the best Soviet defenses could react. On the other hand, the Air Force doubts that the subsonic cruise armed decoy (SCAD) could penetrate terminal defenses, primarily because of its subsonic speed.[9] Hence U.S. bombers would rely on SRAM to suppress terminal defenses that could not be avoided by circumnavigation.

Knowledge of the precise location of the SAM site is essential for targeting the SRAM. If the defenders were to make their SAM systems mobile (at additional costs in money and operational problems), the problem of suppressing the defenses by means of SRAM would become very difficult or impossible.

Destruction Potential against the USSR and China

The alert bomber force that would be expected to survive a preemptive strike carries the equivalent of a thousand 1 megaton weapons consisting of gravity bombs and air-to-surface missiles. Even under the extremely pessimistic assumption that two-thirds of the alert bombers were lost because of unreliability and enemy air defenses,[10] the more than 300 equivalent mega-

8. See *Military Implications of the Treaty . . . on Limitation of Strategic Offensive Arms*, Senate Hearing, p. 480, for a description of Air Force tactics to be used in penetrating Soviet air defenses.

9. *Fiscal Year 1972 Authorization for Military Procurement, Research and Development, Construction and Real Estate Acquisition for the Safeguard ABM and Reserve Strengths*, Hearings before the Senate Committee on Armed Services, 92 Cong. 1 sess. (1971), Pt. 4, p. 3120.

10. Experience with B-52s in penetrating North Vietnamese air defenses in 1972 puts these assumptions in perspective. Surface-to-air missile defenses in some parts of

tons that still could be delivered would be capable of destroying at least the 200 largest Soviet cities containing 34 percent of the Soviet population. In the case of China, the 300 weapons could destroy 10 percent of the population and from 80 to 90 percent of Chinese industry. (The significant difference in population ratios reflects the demographic characteristics discussed in Chapter 2.) Thus, even under very conservative assumptions the U.S. bomber force is capable of inflicting substantial damage on the cities and industrial base of either the USSR or China—a capability independent of land- or sea-based missiles.

As a deterrent against China, U.S. bombers have two advantages over ICBMs. First, it should be possible to reuse them in a war with China. Because Chinese air defenses are relatively weak, the present B-52 force should be able to penetrate and return with impunity. Thus each plane could be counted on for several missions; it would be unnecessary to expend missiles, which are not easily replaced in the short run. Second, bombers would not have to overfly the Soviet Union in attacking China, as would American ICBMs. Of course, U.S. Polaris/Poseidon missiles could also be launched against China without overflight problems.

North Vietnam were reported to be the most dense of any deployed in the world; their crews were experienced and alerted by repeated raids. Although the B-52s penetrated at medium altitudes most favorable to the defense, their electronic countermeasures were so effective that the attrition was only 3 percent. While that rate would be considered high in a continuing conventional war, it would be small for a single strategic strike. Fighter/interceptors did not participate as they probably would over the USSR or China; however, they would be susceptible to the same electronic countermeasures.

Cost Definitions

Projections of the aggregate cost of the strategic force and of its major components are based on a fourfold classification of defense costs, as is explained in the following paragraphs. A similar method was used in preparing the defense cost projections in Charles L. Schultze and others, *Setting National Priorities: The 1974 Budget* (Brookings Institution, 1973).

Major System Acquisition Costs

Annual estimates were made of operational strategic force levels and the amount of funds to be allocated to the research and development, procurement, and military construction related to a limited number of strategic systems. These projections were based on unit cost data, schedules, and development costs reported in various Department of Defense publications and in the congressional testimony of Defense Department officials. Hearings held by the Senate Armed Services Committee were particularly useful.

The systems that were projected explicitly included the strategic bomber force (bomber aircraft, tanker aircraft, and air-to-surface missiles), land-based systems (launchers and missiles, with funds for silo modification projected separately), sea-based systems (submarines, missiles, and base construction), missile defenses (Safeguard and Site Defense of Minuteman), and air defenses (interceptor aircraft squadrons, surface-to-air missile batteries, radar sites, control centers, and warning and control aircraft).

The projection of major system acquisition costs incorporated three steps:

• A baseline projection was made, founded solely on Defense Department estimates of program costs prepared for the fiscal 1972 and 1973 congressional budget hearings.

• Next, an allowance was added for real growth in the cost of new weapons (as opposed to cost increases attributable to inflation). Real cost growth occurs because of uncertainties in predicting the cost of new technologies, changes in performance requirements made during development, and the incentives for lower cost estimates inherent in the U.S. budgetary process before procurement is approved. The two most important factors determining the amount of real cost growth likely to be associated with a particular system are the length of time before the system is scheduled to become operational and the degree of technological advance incorporated in its design. Over the past fifteen years or so, major U.S. weapon systems have consistently exhibited real cost growth averaging 40 percent above the estimates made when system development was authorized.[1]

• Lastly, an allowance was made for new initiatives later in the decade that are not now considered part of the official strategic program. This allowance compensates in part for the so-called tail-off effect implicit in any long-range projection such as this. As current programs are completed, the resources that are freed come under pressure for commitment to new programs that currently are deferred or understated.

In total, we project a real increase of $9 billion (30 percent) arising from obligations for major strategic systems between fiscal 1974 and 1980. About half this amount is traceable to the Trident system; another 30 percent is attributable to the B-1. Only a part of the $9 billion increase will be included in the defense budget before fiscal 1981, however. We estimate this portion to be roughly 60 percent of real cost growth, or $5.7 billion; the balance would affect the defense budget from fiscal 1981 through 1984.

The allowance for new initiatives totaled $1.1 billion and was distributed over the period fiscal 1977 through 1980. Programs that could necessitate this spending include procurement of SAM-D for strategic defense, development and procurement of a new tanker for the B-1, and full-scale development of mobile ICBMs.

The allowances for cost growth and new initiatives are estimated to add the following amounts to major system acquisition costs (total obligational authority in billions of fiscal 1974 dollars):

1. Robert Perry and others, *System Acquisition Strategies*, Report R-733-PR/ARPA (Santa Monica: RAND, June 1971); Comptroller General of the United States, "Cost Growth in Major Weapon Systems" (March 26, 1973; processed).

Fiscal year

	1974	1975	1976	1977	1978	1979	1980
Baseline projection of major system acquisition costs	4.5	4.8	5.7	5.0	4.6	4.2	4.1
Allowance for real cost growth	0	0.2	0.5	1.1	1.2	1.4	1.4
Allowance for new initiatives	0	0	0	0.1	0.2	0.4	0.4
Total	4.5	5.0	6.2	6.2	6.0	6.0	5.9

Other Investment Costs

This category includes the remainder of the research and development, procurement, and military construction appropriations attributable to strategic forces—those not directly related to the acquisition of major weapon systems. Procurement funds in this category are used for such things as test equipment, repair parts, ground support equipment, communications gear, and so forth. The strategic force's share of these expenses, as well as the distribution of costs among the major components of the strategic force, were determined by examining each procurement appropriation in detail. Real cost growth of 5 percent, or $800 million, was assumed to be associated with these expenditures.

Research and development funds in this category are used for basic research on rocket technology, the preliminary design of advanced reentry vehicles, and similar studies of strategic problems. In making the projections, total research and development expenditures were assumed to be fixed. As research expenses for major systems declined, an increased amount was assumed to be spent for basic research. This also helped compensate for the so-called tail-off effect—the difficulty of predicting new initiatives in future years.

Direct Operating Costs

This category includes the military personnel and operations and maintenance costs directly attributable to deployed strategic forces or to their immediate support facilities. Direct support includes such expenses as B-52 squadron operations, Strategic Air Command (SAC) base operations, and the cost of operating SAC command and control—in short, those elements of the military personnel and operations and maintenance appropriations that are funded within Program I (strategic forces) of the Defense Department's Five Year Defense Program. This category also includes the portion of the National Guard and Air National Guard military personnel and operations and maintenance appropriations that is attributable to strategic air defense forces. Hearings held by the Senate and House Appropriations Committees were most helpful in determining direct operating costs.

Indirect Operating Costs

This category, the most contentious one, includes the operating costs of intelligence and communications systems, supply, training, medical care, and administration that are not directly linked to operational forces, but that are necessary for the operational force to perform its mission. These expenditures are usually funded in Programs III, VII, VIII, and IX of the Five Year Defense Program. It was assumed that indirect operating costs attributable to strategic forces, and their distribution among components of the strategic force, are directly proportional to direct operating costs. Thus the bomber force, which is quite costly in terms of manpower and other operational expenses, was assumed to incur a proportionately large share of training expenses, and so forth.

This method of allocating indirect costs to each strategic element is an attempt to simplify a complex and poorly defined relationship, and it has inherent limitations. Some parts of these costs are relatively constant. For example, fairly substantial changes could be made in strategic missile force levels without altering administrative expenses. Nonetheless, since the precise relationship between direct and indirect operating costs is not known and in fact is a matter of some contention, the assumption used here seems at least as valid as any other.